PRAISE FOR
CUSTOMERS INCLUDED
SECOND EDITION

"*Customers Included* is chock-full of fascinating real-world business stories and lessons, each of which illustrates the enduring power of the single greatest business principle ever created: the Golden Rule. And if you wouldn't practice that on your customers, with whom would you?!"
— **Danny Meyer**, Author, *Setting the Table: The Transforming Power of Hospitality in Business*

"*Customers Included* shows how to bake a customer focus into your organization from the get-go. This perspective has been integral to the success of DuckDuckGo, helping us scale and stay relevant. Any entrepreneur who's about to launch a startup should read this book first."
— **Gabriel Weinberg**, Founder and CEO, DuckDuckGo

"Mark Hurst shares some eye-opening examples that point to the real importance of considering, and including, the customer in organizational decisions. *Customers Included* will be a useful resource for the non-profit community."
— **Jilly Stephens**, Executive Director, City Harvest

"Mark Hurst is a true pioneer in customer experience design. In *Customers Included* he shows his uncanny ability to identify and deconstruct what makes for great—and not so great—experiences."
— **Tom X. Lee**, M.D., Founder & CEO, One Medical

"Crafting a high-quality product requires care and respect for those who will use it (or drink it!). I recommend 'popping the cork' on *Customers Included* and drinking up its wisdom."
— **John Williams**, Owner/Winemaker, Frog's Leap Winery

"*Customers Included* is a must-read for product managers who want to build products that customers will be delighted to use again and again."
— **David Yong**, Head of Product, AirAsia Expedia

CUSTOMERS INCLUDED

CUSTOMERS INCLUDED

How to transform products, companies,
and the world — with a single step

SECOND EDITION

MARK HURST

Published in the United States by Creative Good, Inc., New York.
www.creativegood.com

ISBN: 978-0-9793681-3-4

Printed in the United States of America

Cover photo: Terry Border
www.terryborder.com

Cover and book design: The Tremendousness Collective
www.tremendo.us

Author photo: Alice Tan

Typography: *Customers Included* is set in Scala and DIN.

To customers everywhere

TABLE OF CONTENTS

As marketing requested it.

As sales ordered it.

As engineering designed it.

What was manufactured.

What was installed.

What the customer wanted.

INTRODUCTION

W hy do companies so often fail to give customers what they want? The problem is depicted well in the cartoon shown at left. The company pursues a series of unwieldy, unworkable ideas while overlooking the customer's desire for a simple, effective product. The problem could have been avoided, the cartoon suggests, had the company just listened to the customer.

What that might mean in practice is hard to say. How, exactly, is a company supposed to "listen" to its customers? Isn't it the case that customers often don't know what they want? And even if a company did somehow figure out what customers wanted, what would be the next step?

This book responds to those questions by describing a new way for companies to create products, services, and strategies. I call it "customers included," and it makes one simple but radical proposition: When making a decision that affects customers, it's better to *include* customers in that decision, in some meaningful way, rather than completely ignoring them.

It may not seem that there needs to be an entire book written about this idea. After all, what executive plans to ignore customers in a major strategic decision he's about to make? What product manager seeks to leave customers out of the design process as her team develops a new app?

And yet it happens. People appreciate the cartoon on the left because it rings true. After 18 years of consulting to hundreds of companies, I can tell you that ignoring customers is hardly a rarity in the business world. To the contrary, it's the standard way decisions are made and products are created—in every industry, every geography, and every market. There are exceptions, of course, and several are spotlighted in this book. (What's more, the exceptions tend to become the top performers of their industries.) But to most organizations, the "customers included" worldview is anything but business as usual.

It's very important to clarify, however, that this is not a call for companies to become "customer-centered." As popular as this buzzword is, I've never found it to be very realistic. Customers are vitally important but they're not the center of the company. Executives have many other concerns—new technologies, competitive threats, market trends, internal politics—to weigh when charting the organization's strategy. Customers are one of many essential inputs to any significant decision.

But even though customers aren't the center, they also should not be left out of the process entirely. This is where many companies have erred. Concluding (correctly) that it's impossible to be customer-centered, some executives have settled on the other extreme and stopped including customers at all. When I ask why, I usually hear one or more of the following:

- There's not enough time in the project to spend with customers.
- Customers don't know what they want.
- We already know what customers want.
- Customers aren't designers, so we shouldn't ask them to design the product.
- First we need to launch our product, and then we'll find out what customers think.

It's not hard to empathize with each of these. Time is often short, teams often already know what they want to build, and customers indeed should not be asked to design (that's the team's job). But none of these factors should prevent the company from including customers. Customers are an *essential*, not optional, component in the decision-making process. Leaving them out, as we'll see in a number of case studies, can have serious consequences.

Fortunately, there are organizations today that demonstrate a different approach. They create new products, and new strategies, with customers included—not as the center, but as one of several essential ingredients in the process. These organizations have dramatically improved the customer experience in fields as diverse as health care, banking, travel, restaurants, Internet services, urban design, global development, and consumer technology. These case studies, all of which are covered later in the book, point to the effectiveness of this one simple idea: by including customers, organizations can dramatically improve the odds of success for any service, product, innovation, or strategy.

Note that this book uses the word "customer" in a broad sense, denoting anyone on the receiving end of a product, service, or other experience. The customer could be a shopper, a user, a student, a patient, a citizen, or even an employee using an internal service. Every product, every service, every mobile app and website, every innovation of any type has customers. (The use of the word "customer" in this way goes back to 20th century management theorist and author Peter Drucker, about whom I'll say much more, later in the book.)

In all cases, including customers requires three basic steps:
- Observe customers directly.
- Discover customers' key unmet needs.
- Build consensus across the organization to meet those needs.

The book is roughly organized around those three topics. Part 1 covers customers, Part 2 covers research methods (with special emphasis on discovering unmet needs), and Part 3 discusses the organization.

This book is intended to help organizations and teams create better products, services, and experiences for their customers. CEOs, executive directors, general managers, and other leaders are my primary audience, since they are best positioned to change their organizations—and industries—for the better. Product managers, designers, marketers, technologists, and students preparing to take on these roles can also learn from the case studies within these pages.

ABOUT CREATIVE GOOD

Creative Good is a consulting and services firm based in New York City. When I founded the company in 1997, very few people were talking about customer experience; since then, Creative Good has pioneered the discipline and is a world leader in the field. Today, we still maintain our strategic perspective of improving business by improving the customer experience. Part strategy, part organizational development, and part user experience design, our "customers included" worldview remains unique—and uniquely powerful.

Over the past 18 years, Creative Good has worked with hundreds of companies, observed customers on five continents, and developed customer experience strategies for banks, retailers, media companies, and social networks. We've even helped rethink the visitor experience of a city park (more on that later).

After working with this wide range of clients, I can report that the "customers included" approach is universally effective: by observing customers, finding out what customers want, and building organizational consensus, we help our clients deliver the *right* solution. Whether an organization wants to achieve better innovation, higher profits, or some other measurable outcome, including the customer leads to success.

It's worth acknowledging upfront that including customers is hard work. There is no trendy idea or framework that will magically solve the challenges that companies face. The "customers included" process is simple to describe and easy to understand, but it requires real commitment from the team to see the results. With the right people on board, teams can generate incredible results, as I'll describe in later chapters.

First, however, I'll describe what happens—all too commonly—when an organization makes a strategic decision without including the customer.

PART 1

THE CUSTOMER

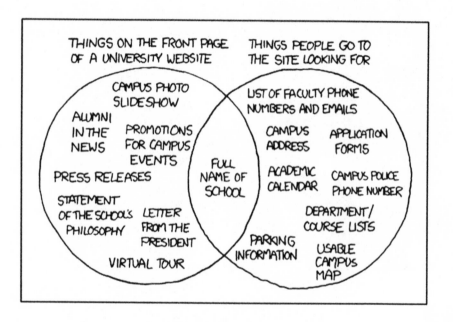

Randall Munroe / xkcd.com

1

THE COST OF IGNORING THE CUSTOMER

"It's a huge mistake."

The driving distance from Los Angeles to Chicago is just over 2,000 miles, requiring about 30 hours to complete. The border between the United States and Mexico, stretching from Tijuana to the Gulf of Mexico, is about the same distance. Securing a national border of such massive length is difficult and expensive, to put it lightly, as shown by the U.S. government's many attempts over the years. One recent failure underscores the importance of including customers in the design process.

A few years ago, the Department of Homeland Security launched a project that promised an innovative approach to decreasing illegal border crossings. The Secure Border Initiative, or SBInet, promised to use technology to deliver more effective results, at lower cost, than previous attempts to secure the border. Boeing, having won the contract to build the system, stood to make billions of dollars if the project succeeded.

It was an ambitious idea. In contrast to a physical fence, which had already been tried at great expense, SBInet would be a "virtual fence," using a high-tech network of sensors, cameras, and surveillance towers to detect crossing attempts. The location of any such attempt would be transmitted to U.S. Border Patrol agents, who would use the data in their ground operations. The effectiveness of the entire system depended on the accuracy of the data and the Border Patrol agents' ability to use it.

An SBInet tower. (U.S. Customs and Border Protection)

Unfortunately, SBInet failed on both counts. When, after numerous schedule delays, a pilot project finally launched on a stretch of the Arizona border, major problems quickly became apparent. The sensors, which had been promised to detect people from miles away, would instead mistake windblown leaves, or even raindrops, for humans. There were more problems in the Border Patrol vehicles, which had been outfitted with laptops for agents to access the sensor data. The laptops, not equipped to work in the dusty environment of the desert, were prone to breakdowns—and even when they were working, Border Patrol agents had difficulty using them while driving on rough terrain.

One might reasonably wonder why the project launched with such obvious flaws. Specifically, why didn't Border Patrol agents raise concerns about the dust and the bumpy roads *before* the system was built and launched?

The answer comes from a Government Accountability Office (GAO) report published in early 2008, a little over a year after Boeing began work on the project. The report concludes that SBInet was "designed and developed by Boeing with minimal input from the intended operators of the system . . . The lack of user involvement resulted in a system that does not fully address or satisfy user needs." Border Patrol agents interviewed for the report said that "the final system might have been more useful if they and others had been given an opportunity to provide feedback."

The customers, in other words, had not been included. Had they been given a voice in the project before it launched, Border Patrol agents almost certainly would have pointed out that laptop computers are not easily used while driving off-road at high speed.

Citing "serious questions about the system's ability to meet the needs for technology along the border," the federal government shut down SBInet in early 2011. Around the same time, in a rare display of bipartisanship, members of Congress from both parties showed their exasperation with the project. This included Arizona's own senator John McCain, who called the virtual fence "a complete failure."

Near the end of the project, the TV program "60 Minutes" sent host Steve Kroft to Arizona to interview the head of SBInet, a man named Mark Borkowski. What followed was a surprisingly frank assessment from a government official:

> Kroft: I'm just kind of amazed that they're building this, what's gonna be a multi-billion dollar system for the Border Patrol, and nobody asked the Border Patrol what they needed or wanted, or what would be helpful . . . that's a pretty big mistake.
>
> Borkowski: It's a huge mistake, it's a huge mistake.

"Huge" is right. By the time SBInet was shut down, the project had cost taxpayers almost a billion dollars. It was an expensive lesson in why customers shouldn't be ignored.

When SBInet officials were asked why they didn't make a point of finding out what Border Patrol agents needed, they told the GAO that

> there was not enough time built into the contract to obtain feedback from all of the intended users of the system during its design and development.

There hadn't been enough time to include the customer. And that may have been factually correct: the phases of the project may have been dictated by contracts, timelines, regulations, and other constraints, preventing anyone from sitting down with agents to understand what they needed. It's unclear who, or what, was ultimately at fault. What's clear is that a huge amount of taxpayer money was wasted because customers had not been properly included.

Two years later, American taxpayers saw yet another problematic launch, this time of Healthcare.gov. Instead of allowing taxpayers to shop for health insurance coverage, the site presented users with a confusing interface and an endless series of technical problems, including going offline altogether. Congressional hearings held in the wake of the launch revealed that Healthcare.gov hadn't been tested with actual users until a few days before it went online. (A Medicare official said that this was "due to a compressed time frame.") Although Healthcare.gov was a very different kind of project from the border fence, the similarities were striking: both were high-profile and expensive government projects that failed to make time to include the customer.

Was the SBInet failure instructive to corporations working to secure the border? Around the time SBInet was shut down, Boeing's competitor Raytheon presented at an industry conference on border security. Raytheon had bid originally on the SBInet project and lost to Boeing, and it was clearly aware of Boeing's troubles. The presenter explained that Raytheon's solution to border security was superior because "Raytheon's software is capable of not only seeing who's approaching the border, but monitoring their movements [and] correlating thousands of pieces of ever-changing data." In other words, Raytheon promised to pack even more technology into the solution than Boeing had. Left out was any indication of whether, or how, Raytheon would fix the central error of Boeing's system. There was no mention of including the customer.

NETFLIX'S MISTAKE OF "TERRIFIC VALUE"

Examples of organizations ignoring the customer are hardly limited to big government programs like the border fence. Even in the fast-moving world of Internet companies, this kind of mistake is surprisingly common. Netflix provides a perfect example of ignoring customers in a key strategic decision.

June 2011 was a peak moment for Netflix. The company's familiar red envelopes carried DVDs to the mailboxes of millions of subscribers across North America. Customers also enjoyed a growing library of movies and TV shows offered by the company's online streaming service. Business was growing and the stock price was at an all-time high. Meanwhile, Netflix's longtime rival Blockbuster had declared bankruptcy. The video-rental chain had long been resented by customers for its late fees—in essence, profiting by punishing customers—and Netflix, the customer-friendly alternative, had won.

Then it all changed. On July 12, 2011, without prior warning, Netflix announced a 60% increase in its monthly subscription price, saying it would "better reflect the costs" of providing the service. There was no mention of any benefit for customers; to the contrary, the higher prices were described as a "terrific value." The reaction from customers was vociferously negative, and many canceled their accounts in protest. (A more amusing reaction came from Jason Alexander, of "Seinfeld" fame, who appeared in a comic video asking for donations to a "Netflix Relief Fund.")

A few weeks later, in an attempt to recover from the mistake, CEO Reed Hastings sent a follow-up message to the entire Netflix customer base. This message was even worse than the first. After a cursory apology for "messing up," Hastings stated that the price rise would stand, and then abruptly announced that Netflix would stop offering DVD rentals at all. Instead, customers would have to open a separate account with a spinoff company named "Qwikster."

Netflix, long known for its simple, easy-to-use service, was now proposing to make things difficult for customers. Checking the availability of a given movie would now require searching two separate websites with two separate accounts. Combined with the recent price increase, this announcement understandably angered customers.

What resulted was one of the loudest and most sustained complaints from any company's customers, ever. Torrents of negative response poured out of Twitter, Facebook, and blogs—including Netflix's own blog, which got thousands of outraged comments. Even "Saturday Night Live" ridiculed Qwikster with a skit showing Reed Hastings announcing several more new names for its service.

Within a month, Netflix retracted the plan for the Qwikster spinoff, writing in a blog post that "it is clear that for many of our members two websites would make things more difficult." Indeed. Netflix had finally listened to customers, but not before its reputation had taken an enormous hit. Previously seen as a customer-friendly alternative to Blockbuster, now Netflix appeared to be similarly willing to gouge its subscribers.

Why would a company with a spotless reputation voluntarily do something to antagonize millions of customers? Shortly after the Qwikster plan was scrapped, Reed Hastings told a reporter that he had made "a mistake in underestimating the depth of emotional attachment to Netflix." That's a fair assessment, though it is important to clarify where that emotional attachment came from.

In the countless research sessions my team has conducted at Creative Good, observing customers interact with mobile apps, websites, and other experiences, I can't remember a single instance in which someone expressed an emotional attachment to a logo, a color, or a slogan. Instead, customers respond to the *benefits* they get from the experience. If a company offers a good enough customer experience—in which, yes, the logo and other "branding elements" play supporting roles—then customers may eventually form an emotional attachment to the brand.

This was indeed the case with Netflix. Customers' emotional attachment came directly from the convenience and ease-of-use of the service. Netflix's brand was (and still is) fully defined by the experience it creates for customers. Hastings' mistake may be summed up in a simple rule of thumb: Harm the customer experience and you harm the company.

Unhappy with the pricing change and the Qwikster debacle, around 800,000 Netflix customers canceled their accounts in a period of a few months. The company's stock price also suffered, going from a high of $298 around the time of the first email to a low of $54 about a year later. For both Netflix and the border fence, ignoring customers was an incredibly expensive mistake.

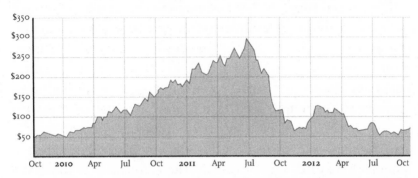

Netflix stock price, October 2009 to October 2012.

An essay by Farhad Manjoo in *Slate*, however, argued that Hastings had actually made the *right* decision, despite customers' overwhelmingly negative reaction, pronouncing that "the problem with customers is that they don't always know what's best for them." Manjoo went on to give Hastings one of the highest compliments in the technology industry, saying his actions were "disruptive." The idea that innovators should ignore the customer in an attempt to be disruptive is unfortunately a common misunderstanding and bears some explaining.

ON DISRUPTIVE INNOVATION

The term "disruption" was popularized in *The Innovator's Dilemma*, a 1997 book by Harvard Business School professor Clayton Christensen. The book features case studies of several industries, from hard drives to mechanical excavators, that were "disrupted"—that is, transformed by the arrival of radically new technologies.

The history of the technology industry is filled with disruptive change: think of DEC and Wang's minicomputers being replaced by PCs, or personal digital assistants (PDAs) like the Palm Treo being steamrolled by the Apple iPhone. In each case, the incumbent product would not have been saved by an incrementally better interface—with a higher-resolution screen, say, or slightly better usability. A disruptive competitor reorients the market around itself, while the older product quickly becomes irrelevant.

Christensen suggests that listening to one's current customers may cause a company to limit itself to "sustaining technologies," thus preserving its current business while ignoring the larger competitive landscape. Paying too much attention to today's customers, he warns, could lead a company to avoid the necessary step of disrupting *itself* to prepare for tomorrow's market. The inevitable arrival of a disruptive competitor could then be fatal, despite—or even because of—the company's interest in its customers. As Christensen puts it, "There are times at which it is right *not* to listen to customers."

In Netflix's case, one could argue that the DVDs-by-mail business was under disruptive threat from online streaming. Banishing the DVDs to a (clumsily named) spinoff would firmly establish Netflix's future as a streaming business. Of course, customers would complain at first—customers naturally resist change—but in time they would come to appreciate the shift. In other words, one could argue, it would be unwise to listen to the customer.

This line of thinking almost killed Netflix. Like the border fence project, Netflix plunged ahead with a strategy that ignored the customer, and it suffered the painful result. In both cases it would have been far better to consider customers' needs during the decision process. With even a small amount of research, for example, Reed Hastings could have discovered how much customers valued Netflix's ease-of-use. He could have then formed a strategy of pursuing the disruption (focusing more on streaming) while avoiding the spinoff of a second service, thereby preserving the single, easy interface that customers loved. Instead, Hastings attempted to radically transform Netflix without regard for how it affected people outside the company: a mistake, he said later, stemming from "arrogance based upon past success." Things might have gone much differently had Hastings considered the customer as an essential input to the decision.

Unfortunately, in an effort to be "disruptive," many entrepreneurs have concluded that they should ignore customers altogether. This view is largely supported by the business press, which rarely mentions customers when it discusses disruption. For example, the *Economist* recently described disruptive innovation as "capturing new markets by embracing new technologies and adopting new business models." It's no accident that the word "new" appears three times—and that customers aren't mentioned at all. As disruptive innovation is widely understood, what's important is that it's creating something *new*, not that it's actually creating a better experience for customers. Ironically, the *Economist* article goes on to cite Netflix as an example of disruption, in its shift to "streaming on-demand video to its customers." There's no mention of how this strategy, as initially carried out, excluded customers and harmed the company.

The current trend to pursue anything that can be called "disruptive" can tempt executives to make high-profile mistakes on par with Qwikster. This is the case made by Jill Lepore in a 2014 *New Yorker* article, "The Disruption Machine," in which she explores "what the gospel of innovation gets wrong." After taking a critical look at Christensen's original case studies, Lepore concludes that "much of the theory of disruptive innovation rests on [an] arbitrary definition of success," pointing out that many of the "disruptive" companies praised in the case studies enjoyed "fleeting success" but today are no longer in business—while the companies that were supposedly disrupted by those leaner, more agile competitors are still active and profitable. Along the same lines, strategist Ben Thompson points out that Christensen has repeatedly predicted that the iPhone would be disrupted by cheaper Android devices. As shown by Apple's record-breaking profits in early 2015, that hasn't yet occurred. (I'll cover Apple in more detail in Chapter 3.)

I'm not suggesting that the theory of disruption is invalid, since it does of course occur and can be achieved by smart teams. I merely want to point out that attempts at disruption have a better chance of succeeding when they include the customer. In other words, pursuing disruption *by itself* is not sufficient to create a winning strategy. One could propose a dozen ways to disrupt any given industry, but without some thought toward the impact on customers, all those disruptive ideas are likely to fail. Companies that aim to be disruptive should include, not ignore, the customer.

NETFLIX'S RECOVERY

Fortunately for fans of movies and TV shows, Netflix's missteps weren't fatal. Instead, Hastings used the crisis as an opportunity to get back to basics and refocus the company on the customer experience. As a result, by summer 2013, Netflix had largely recovered from the crisis, with the stock price advancing past $200 for the first time since the events of July 2011. (As of this writing, in March 2015, Netflix is trading at over $400 per share.)

When asked how he guided Netflix back to health, Hastings said that "there was amazing pressure to come up with the shiny object that would make everything better—but the phrase I used was, 'There are no shortcuts.'" A "steady and disciplined" focus enabled Netflix to "execute on the fundamentals"—that is, provide a good experience for customers.

Reed Hastings deserves credit for recovering from his mistakes; seeing the world through the eyes of a customer is not always easy. Yet it is vitally important. A team can amass all the money, talent, and technology in the world, but without also considering the customer's perspective, any innovation risks failure. A good example of this can be seen in the next chapter.

CHAPTER 1 SUMMARY

This chapter establishes what can happen when organizations ignore the customer. This mistake, and its consequences, can occur in organizations of all types, from government agencies to Internet companies.

KEY POINTS

- It can be expensive to ignore the customer. After spending a billion dollars on SBInet, the government shut down the project—which hadn't adequately involved the agents who would use the system— and declared it a "complete failure."
- Netflix paid a steep price for jeopardizing the ease-of-use and convenience that customers so highly valued. The company later recovered by focusing on the basics of the customer experience.
- "Disruptive innovation" can be a helpful framework for understanding a fast-moving competitive environment like the technology industry. However, focusing only on disruptive forces, to the exclusion of concern for the customer, is a dangerous strategy. Even in disruptive environments, it is still essential to include the customer.

2

INNOVATION MISSING ONE INGREDIENT

"They didn't ask us."

M any African villages contain a hand pump that the community relies on for its water. Usually pumped by women, the water is then used for drinking, cooking, and bathing. If a village doesn't have a pump, the women (and, often enough, girls) might walk miles to the nearest water source. Throughout the region, countless lives would be improved, or even saved, with better access to clean drinking water.

In 2005, news arrived of a promising new South African invention called the Playpump. Essentially a merry-go-round with a pump hidden inside, the device used children's normal play activity to pump underground water into a nearby storage tank. A televised report from PBS showed the Playpump in action: a group of smiling children spun rapidly on a brightly colored roundabout as water gushed from a tap.

The Playpump business model was equally inventive. The storage tank sat several meters high and could display several large billboards. Advertising revenue would pay for ongoing maintenance of the pump. With a single Playpump installation, children would get new playground equipment, residents would have easy access to clean water, and because of the billboards, it would all be free.

The reception to the Playpump was immediate and enthusiastic. A PBS webpage accompanying the TV story received hundreds of supportive comments from viewers. More media coverage followed, including a *Time* magazine column by former president Bill Clinton and a video by *National Geographic*. And in 2007, the Playpump was nominated for a National Design Award by the Cooper-Hewitt National Design Museum.

A Playpump in action. (Playpumps International)

Perhaps the most important outcome of the PBS piece was the financial support it helped generate. At the Clinton Global Initiative in September 2006, First Lady Laura Bush announced a $16.4 million investment in Playpumps—including $10 million from the U.S. government and $5 million from the foundation of Steve Case, founder of AOL. Around the same time, popular hip-hop artist Jay-Z raised $250,000 for Playpumps at a concert in New York City.

At this stage Playpump had everything that entrepreneurs dream of: an attractive product, enthusiastic press, plenty of money, and

A-list support from politicians, business leaders, and celebrities. With this impressive momentum established, the company behind the effort, Playpumps International, went to work bringing Playpumps to dozens of locations in Africa.

But the Playpump failed. By May 2010, the Case Foundation publicly announced that it would no longer support the project. The remaining inventory of Playpumps was transferred to another organization to install for limited uses. This abrupt outcome might seem strange for a project that appeared to have so much potential. But for the people in the villages, there was no mystery about what had gone wrong.

Around the time the Case Foundation withdrew its support, a young Canadian aid worker in Malawi named Owen Scott posted a five-minute video on YouTube. The video shows another aid worker, Duncan McNicholl, spinning a Playpump as fast as he can, while water flows into a bucket. He stops when the bucket is full. "Total time: 3:07," reads the caption. The video then shows McNicholl using a traditional hand-operated pump. The bucket quickly fills up. "Total time: 0:28." The Playpump took six times as long as the hand pump.

There had been earlier indications of problems with the Playpump, and not just due to its poor efficiency. In 2008 the Mozambique government commissioned an independent research agency to evaluate one hundred Playpump installations in the country. The results were grim: many of the Playpumps were not working when researchers arrived, and the mean time for repair of a faulty pump was sixty days—a long time to wait when water is already scarce. In the words of the report, "The downtime of some of the Playpumps (some never even worked) is a real disaster for all stakeholders, especially for the communities in need of water."

Even functioning Playpumps presented a problem, as children were unable to keep up the constant spinning needed to draw much water. In one evocative passage, the report describes how children were willing to play for the benefit of foreign visitors, but soon tired:

In most schools visited, children were not always moving the play wheel—they often enjoyed the Playpump as a gathering place, just sitting on it and chatting.

However, as soon as the evaluation team (foreigners) walked towards the Playpump, the children rushed to the pump (like they have been told), showing their ability to rotate the play wheel at an enormous speed. The children pushing the wheel with such a high speed could only keep up this pace for a few minutes before being exhausted. For smaller children and mainly girls just sitting on the pump, one minute of constant rotation was enough for them to leave the pump before getting dizzy.

There were thus a number of difficulties with Playpumps: they didn't pump water efficiently, they broke down a lot, and kids were not able to pump much water without getting dizzy. But there was an even more serious problem. The Mozambique report describes it: "Most of the pumps were installed on existing operational bore-holes." In other words, an existing working pump was ripped out of the ground, only to be replaced by the Playpump. Owen Scott, the aid worker in Malawi mentioned earlier, interviewed the teachers of his village about the day they got their Playpump. The video, which he posted on YouTube, includes this exchange:

Teacher: And the borehole it was all right, and all of a sudden, they came, a certain organization, to replace that borehole with the Playpump.

Scott: Did they ask you before they replaced it?

Teacher: No, they didn't ask us. Just come and say that we are going to replace this borehole with this Playpump because . . . they said the government invited these Playpumps from South Africa, so we want to try these here in Malawi.

In villages all across the region, people had seen their water source taken away—and replaced with a merry-go-round.

Now the problems listed earlier take on new significance. The

Playpump's inefficiency, taking six times as long as the hand pump, was crucial—because this was now the only pump in the village. And when kids became dizzy after a minute of spinning, it was up to the adults to step in. Owen Scott observed that "when children don't play enough to fill the watertank on a Playpump, women are left spinning the wheel manually to draw water." The Mozambique report notes that "it turned out to be very heavy for women to operate the [Playpump]." For "pregnant women, elderly, disabled, and sick people," it was impossible.

The maintenance issues were especially problematic, because when the Playpump broke down, no one had the tools or the training to fix it, and then there was *no* pump in the village. This was the disheartening finding of the PBS reporter—the same one who had filed the 2005 piece—when she returned to Africa in 2010 to see the results of the Playpump project. She observed:

> I met women who had been without their own supply of clean drinking water for months, because their Playpump had broken down and had never been repaired or replaced.

There wasn't much the community could do in response, she said, since the residents "were stripped of their task to organize and maintain" the pump. Once the Playpump broke down, the women would have to pick up their buckets and start walking.

WHY THE PLAYPUMP FAILED

In all three case studies covered so far (border fence, Netflix, and Playpump), there is a striking similarity: customers were not adequately involved in a decision that would affect them. Massive amounts of money were wasted—and in the Playpump's case, lives were put at risk—all because customers were not included.

What's more, similar to the GAO reports on the border fence, there was clear documentation of the Playpump team's mistake. The authors of the Mozambique report saw "no signs that communities had been consulted prior to installation." Even earlier, barely a year after the Clinton conference, Unicef issued its own report on the Playpump project, noting that "the Playpumps International implementation strategy lacks adequate community consultation."

Despite having considerable financial backing, and enviable resources in nearly every possible respect, the Playpump leadership made the crucial mistake of ignoring their customer. As a result, U.S. taxpayers effectively paid millions of dollars to *reduce* the availability of clean water in Africa.

It's hard to imagine the Playpump getting funded if those in charge had taken more time to learn the context on the ground. This would have required more than touring a village for an afternoon and having a film crew shoot a few minutes of footage. Owen Scott was able to reveal the Playpump's flaws in his YouTube videos because he had taken time to observe how the community interacted with the pump. It requires a real commitment of time and energy, especially in an unfamiliar context, to include the customer.

INNOVATION FOR THE WRONG AUDIENCE

In a strange way, the Playpump *was* built with customers in mind. It's just that the customers weren't poor Africans. Instead, the design—playful, innovative, aimed at solving a tough problem—was perfectly calibrated to capture the attention of a western audience. This view is advanced by South African researcher Ralph Borland, who wrote his 2011 PhD dissertation on the topic. Borland argues that the Playpump was successful to western audiences for the same reason that it was harmful to end users:

> The Playpump as 'innovative,' which has helped it win awards, is part of its attractive power to observers. But the nature of its innovation targets audiences rather than users . . . The Playpump is an innovative object only in the spectacular, broad brush-strokes way in which innovation is communicated through the press to first world audiences.

Borland concludes that the Playpump "prioritizes benefit to its producers and partners, and the maintenance of its image to audiences, over the needs of users in the developing world." Or as Owen Scott put it, the Playpump "illustrates the triumph of rich-country whimsy over poor-country relevance."

The Playpump is hardly the only global development project that received accolades for its "innovative" solution, despite the problems with its approach. A recent *Foreign Policy* article praises several examples, including the Playpump, as well as something called the Socckett, a $99 soccer ball with an embedded chargeable battery. After kids play with the soccer ball all day (I have to ask: why should children have to play in order to get basic utilities?), the ball can temporarily power an attachable LED lamp. By playing during the day, the idea goes, kids will have a light for doing their schoolwork at night.

I think an even better idea would be for ten kids, not just one, to have lighting for $99. The *Foreign Policy* article points out that a dependable, portable solar-powered lamp costs $10. But that's not the device that influential voices have called "brilliant," "extraordinary," and "revolutionary." Those words were reserved for the Socckett.

THE SPAGHETTI METHOD

Many organizations today aspire to be innovative, or to be perceived as such, yet seem not to fully understand what that might require. The word itself is problematic: "innovation" has been so overused that it's not always clear what people mean when they say it, other than vaguely "doing cool stuff." Some teams thus end up pursuing "cool stuff" with little consideration for how it might affect the larger world. In his book *To Save Everything, Click Here*, Evgeny Morozov explains:

> Innovation is treated as inherently good in itself, regardless of its social or political consequences . . . Since innovation is seen as having only positive effects, few are prepared to examine its unintended consequences; as such, most innovations are presumed to be self-evidently good.

A similar mindset seems to have been present in the Playpump project. Recall that the Case Foundation was a major funder, donating $5 million to the project. Announcing its withdrawal of support when the Playpump's failure became apparent, the Case Foundation published a blog post stating its conclusion about the project. Was it that the strategy hadn't fully understood the context on the ground? Or something about maintenance issues and supply chains? No. Instead, the blog post read:

> The very nature of innovation requires that we try new things and take risks. Sometimes they will work, other times they won't.

In other words, this is just how innovation works: you try a bunch of stuff, some succeeds, some doesn't. Although I don't agree with this conclusion, the argument is common enough that it deserves a closer look.

What the Case Foundation's blog post called "the very nature of innovation" is what would more accurately be called the "spaghetti method": simply put, throw some noodles at the wall and see what sticks. One might also describe it as an evolutionary process, trying many ideas ("variation") and measuring the results to find the best idea ("selection"). Whatever it's called, it is not the "very nature" but rather one of many possible methods of innovation.

Like any other method, there are instances where it works well. The spaghetti method is best employed when there are many available ideas to try, and not much downside for some failures along the way. For example, a venture capital firm may invest in a multitude of startup companies in the hopes that one will strike gold. Here a high failure rate is acceptable, even admirable, since one gigantic success will more than make up for all the duds. This helps explain the Silicon Valley adage to "fail early, fail often." When you're playing the lottery, you need lots of tickets, because most of them will lose.

The spaghetti method becomes problematic, however, when failure is not so acceptable. A major launch can be very expensive if it goes wrong, as shown by Netflix and the border fence. And if the product significantly affects customers' lives, as the Playpump did, failure can bring a cascade of unwanted outcomes. In cases like these, it's reckless to merely choose a novel-sounding idea and "see if it sticks."

There is a widespread misunderstanding today that innovation requires, or equates to, the spaghetti method. It does not. Not every situation calls for throwing ideas against the wall, hoping against hope that something will work. Any company that wants to maximize its chance at a successful innovation should include the customer along the way.

This is not a new idea. Peter Drucker, the legendary management scholar and consultant, wrote over forty years ago that "the measure of innovation is the impact on the environment"—that is, the real-world results it generates (and not how much excitement or press coverage it gets). He grants that many innovations fail, noting that "nine out of ten 'brilliant ideas' turn out to be nonsense," but he is clear about how an innovation team should find the right ideas to pursue. "Often the most direct way," Drucker writes, is to "start out with the consumer's or client's need for a significant change." Even in risky situations, in other words, it's essential to keep the customer in mind.

A BETTER PUMP

For a much better example of innovation in action, let's return once more to sub-Saharan Africa to examine a water pump. Not the Playpump. This is the Zimbabwe bush pump, a reliable and popular hand pump that has provided clean drinking water to African communities for over twenty years. Just as the Playpump failed by ignoring the end user, the Zimbabwe bush pump succeeded by doing just the opposite. It includes customers in two main ways.

First of all, the inventor of the pump, Peter Morgan, based his design on an existing pump in use since the 1930s. Having worked on the ground in Africa for years, Morgan had directly observed how well this pump worked, and he knew what aspects of the construction could be improved (and made more cost-effective). While this may not seem particularly innovative, it shows Morgan's interest in creating a pump that simply worked well—this is Drucker's "impact on the environment"—regardless of how new the design was. In a book on water management, Morgan explains why he started with a familiar design: "As a rule of thumb, it is generally far better to take an existing technology, well established in a particular country, and build on that and develop it, rather than introduce something foreign." By focusing on effectiveness rather than flash, Morgan put users' interests first.

Second, Morgan set an expectation that the community would participate in the installation of its pump. Morgan's book recommends enlisting the help of residents to drill the borehole (and only after calling on a local water diviner to help select a site). The community should also be consulted on the storage of maintenance materials and invited to training sessions on pump operation and repair. It may seem like a lot of activity for a single hand pump, but as Morgan puts it, "without this participation, communities cannot generate the commitment for maintenance as they do when they are involved."

The Zimbabwe bush pump. (Aquamor)

Note how the bush pump treats villagers not as a remote constituency to be kept away from innovation, but as an integral part of the process, from the design phase all the way through installation and ongoing maintenance. Morgan clearly makes the case (and the Playpump demonstrates) that designing a pump is likely to fail without carefully and intentionally including the users. This is indeed the conclusion of two researchers who, in 2000, published a paper about Morgan and his pump. Clearly impressed with what they saw, they make this insightful observation: "The pump is nothing without the community that it will serve." Morgan's bush pump, in other words, can't be understood merely as an assemblage of metal parts. The community is part of the pump, too.

Of course, there are drawbacks to Morgan's approach. The Zimbabwe bush pump has never won a design award, has never received significant media attention, and has not made Morgan famous. Designed purely for the long-term benefit of its users, the pump quietly does its job and doesn't draw attention to itself. Contrast this with award-winning innovations that are built chiefly for the momentary enjoyment of a media audience. The Playpump may have looked great on TV, but that didn't translate to much benefit for African villagers.

The Playpump fits a pattern I've often encountered in my team's consulting work at Creative Good. A client seeks to pursue a trendy, flashy new initiative, while our research discovers that what customers really want is a simple, unadorned solution to their problem. In cases like this, it can be tempting for the client to ignore customers in favor of a more exciting alternative. Nevertheless, we encourage teams to pay attention to the customer and, as Reed Hastings put it, "execute on the fundamentals."

THE AMAZING GOOGLE WAVE

But the shiny object is alluring. All too commonly I see teams, full of smart, educated professionals, chasing after so-called "innovative" ideas at the expense of what customers actually want. This occurs with startling frequency in the technology industry, where companies expend massive resources on products and services that generate only momentary attention by the market. A good example of this was the high-profile, but short-lived, Google Wave.

Google Wave was a web-based service announced in 2009 at Google I/O, the company's annual developers' conference. Reports from the event indicate that developers loved what they saw in the on-stage demo: audience members "stood up and cheered like nothing [they had] seen outside of a Steve Jobs keynote," with one attendee "literally waving his laptop in the air in excitement." Exactly what the audience saw is hard to describe. Google Wave brought together a panoply of features—chat, photos, file sharing, and more—into a single browser window. A user could hold multiple conversations with multiple people in multiple parts of the screen, all at once, communicating and sharing online in a brand new way. Or something like that.

Google Wave. (CrunchBase)

When it launched, Wave presented users with an assortment of chat sessions, user avatars, message editors, photo thumbnails, menus, buttons, links, and other features. To put it plainly, Wave was a mess. It didn't even feel like a Google project, as it deviated from the company's well-known simple aesthetic. And the value of the tool was unclear. No one, not even at Google, seemed to be able to describe what Google Wave *was*, beyond being something new and innovative.

These glaring drawbacks didn't prevent the technology media from immediately heaping praise on Google Wave. TechCrunch called it "very sleek and easy . . . makes email look stale." Mashable said Wave was "slick and easy to navigate . . . more intuitive than email," then in a subsequent review called it "a game changer . . . [Wave] aspires to redefine not only email, but the entire web." Despite these striking assertions, the articles included no observations of people using the tool other than Google employees or the journalists themselves.

Not long afterward, the technology website Ars Technica published a long review of Google Wave, calling it "intriguing," "compelling," "truly audacious," and "highly sophisticated" before launching into an extensive description of the functionality and underlying architecture, finally concluding that Wave was "an extraordinary technical achievement." Whether the tool was something users actually would find helpful, or indeed usable at all, was left unexplored.

Still, customers weren't ignored for long. Much like the Playpump, Google got to see how customers reacted to its new product when it launched publicly. Google sent out thousands of invites to Wave in September 2009, prompting an immediate surge of reviews. Users were unsparing in their feedback, saying what previous reviewers had been unwilling to voice: Google Wave was a confusing, over-engineered, unusable flop.

One of the first widely shared remarks came from Robert Scoble, a popular technology blogger, who noted that "as people start to use [Google Wave] they will realize it brings the worst of email and IM together: unproductivity." A day later, technology commentator Anil

Dash wrote that Google Wave was "like a Segway for email." Talk of Google Wave soon spread far enough into the popular culture that *Newsweek* printed its own review, concluding that "this is what happens when engineers are left unsupervised . . . If the engineers had been left alone for another six months they'd have put in Jedi Knights and Klingons, too."

A few months later, just over a year after launching Wave, Google announced that the service would be shut down. "We have always pursued innovative projects," the post begins (in language strikingly similar to the Case Foundation's post about the "nature of innovation"). Then: "Wave has not seen the user adoption we would have liked." By the time Google finally paid attention to users, it was clear that they weren't using the tool.

The launch of Wave wasn't the last time Google failed to include customers. In early 2013, Google cofounder Sergey Brin went on stage at the TED conference to show off Google Glass, a wearable computer and camera built into eyeglass frames. Comparing his product favorably to the "emasculating" experience of using a smartphone, Brin demonstrated Google Glass's ability to record video of everyone in sight of the device.

Much like Wave, Google Glass enjoyed widespread acclaim in the press—*Time* named it one of the "best inventions of the year"— well before everyday users had a chance to use the device. I saw things differently. Two days after Brin's TED presentation, I wrote a column on the Creative Good blog about "the Google Glass feature no one is talking about"—namely, that anyone within sight of a Glass device could have their likeness, statements, and actions recorded and stored on Google's cloud servers, in perpetuity, with no chance to opt out. The experience of Google Glass, like any other device, would dictate its eventual success or failure. But in this case, I wrote, "the key experiential question of Google Glass isn't what it's like to wear them, it's what it's like to be around someone *else* who's wearing them."

My column apparently struck a chord, as within a few days it went viral, eventually gaining tens of thousands of shares on social media. I was hardly the only person with misgivings about Glass. Journalists began to question the merits of the device, spotlighting concerns raised by privacy advocates. Some bars and movie theaters banned patrons from wearing Glass on the premises. And perhaps inevitably, the device was ridiculed on "Saturday Night Live" (by none other than Fred Armisen, who had also starred in SNL's Netflix skit mentioned in the previous chapter). Google's response throughout this storm of complaint was mostly to stay quiet, except to have PR spokespeople issue an occasional statement saying, in effect, "you'll get used to it."

Although they were very different products, Google Wave and Google Glass suffered from the same mistake: the company didn't sufficiently consider how the product would affect people on the receiving end. Wave was so complicated that no one was quite sure what it *was*. With Glass, Google seemed indifferent to (or even contemptuous of) the desires and fears of everyday people who weren't tech-enabled or wealthy enough to own the device.

In the end, Google paid the price for failing to include the customer. Sales of Google Glass declined as wearing the device became so stigmatized that even Sergey Brin stopped wearing his Glass in public. Finally, in early 2015, Google announced that it was halting sales of Google Glass altogether. "All that fanfare for nothing," wrote Nick Bilton in the *New York Times*. "This wasn't how the story was supposed to end." Yet in hindsight, Google's experience with Wave should have taught the company what can happen when customers aren't properly included.

Google Wave, Google Glass, and the Playpump teach an important lesson: customers will eventually have their say. No amount of initial enthusiasm in the media will shield a company from the reality of the customer experience. A poorly designed pump will eventually break down and leave a village without water. A poorly designed website will be rejected by users. A poorly conceived device will be shut down by public opposition.

Any innovation process that leaves out the customer will suffer the effects when the product launches. It's amazing that some teams actually prefer to innovate in this way. What's more, some teams seem to believe that true innovation *requires* leaving the customer out of the process. This misconception is covered in the next chapter.

CHAPTER 2 SUMMARY

This chapter shows what happens when a team assembles the ingredients of successful innovation but leaves out the customer.

KEY POINTS

- The Playpump demonstrated the risks of innovating without including the customer. Innovation can have real-world effects on the lives of individuals and communities, so it's important to get right.

- A common misconception is that an "innovation" is something clever, playful, or high-tech enough to get press coverage or win design awards.

- Another common misconception is that the innovation process equates to the "spaghetti method." This is not at all the case, and the spaghetti method itself has limited use.

- Peter Morgan revealed a better way of innovating, by focusing on creating benefits for the customer. Similarly, Peter Drucker wrote that innovation must be measured by its impact.

- As Google Wave and Google Glass showed, customers will have their say when an innovation launches. The team must decide whether it wants to include customers before then.

3

STARTING WITH THE CUSTOMER EXPERIENCE

"Mr. Jobs didn't buy into focus groups."

On the east coast, a chain of grocery stores called Stew Leonard's is well known for what sits in every store entrance: a three-ton slab of granite. On the stone is etched the following text:

Our Policy
Rule 1: The customer is always right!
Rule 2: If the customer is ever wrong, reread Rule 1.

The story goes that, just after the opening of the first Stew Leonard's store in 1969, the founder (Stew Leonard himself) was accosted at the entrance by an irate customer complaining about some sour eggnog she had bought there. Stew refunded the purchase, but not before remarking that the eggnog was probably just fine. The customer vowed never to return and stormed off, prompting Stew to make a bold commitment to customer service—literally etching the policy in stone. The customer is always right.

The problem with this philosophy is that, taken to the logical extreme, it's an unattainable ideal. Try walking into Stew Leonard's and announcing that you think a gallon of milk costs a nickel. Are you "right"? No grocery store, no team, no organization would survive long with this mindset. As stated in the introduction, being truly "customer-centered" is an unrealistic goal.

Perhaps sensing the impossibility of that path, some executives seem to aspire to the other extreme: innovating without any customer input at all. I've met plenty of these executives over the years. After calmly explaining that they already know what their customers want, they usually offer up the same two examples. First they quote Henry Ford: "If I had asked people what they wanted, they would have said faster horses." (I try not to mention that there's no evidence that Ford ever said that.) Then, almost without fail, I hear about someone else.

THE MISUNDERSTOOD MR. JOBS

Talk to anyone about including customers and sooner or later the conversation will turn to Steve Jobs. Years after his death, his iconic image lives on: the maverick genius who flouted convention, blazed his own path, and created insanely great products.

Jobs is widely seen as having designed products only for himself. The mythology evokes a lone visionary, thinking up elegant designs that suited his own personal tastes. In this rendering, customers were an afterthought, bit players whose only role was to dutifully buy whatever innovation Jobs conjured up. Apple effectively had only one customer, and he wasn't concerned with pleasing anyone else.

It's an attractive story, but it's wrong. The truth is that customers were central to Jobs' innovation process. Scratch just below the glossy veneer of his legend and you can plainly see how Apple succeeded by including customers. It's a nuanced story that bears some explanation.

One reason people misunderstand Jobs is because of his vocal opposition to traditional consumer research. As early as 1989, Jobs told an interviewer, "You can't just ask customers what they want and then try to give that to them. They rarely wind up getting what they really want that way." In a later interview he was even more direct: "People don't know what they want until you show it to them."

Near the end of his life, as journalists attempted to summarize his career, Jobs was repeatedly described as spurning customer input.

The *New York Times* reported that Jobs was "uncompromising . . . prototypes are shown not to focus groups or other outsiders, but to Mr. Jobs and a few members of his team." After Jobs died, the *Times'* David Pogue wrote:

> [Apple has] had stunningly few flops. And that's because Mr. Jobs didn't buy into focus groups, groupthink or decision by committee. He oversaw every button, every corner, every chime.

The message was loud and clear: Jobs didn't like involving outsiders, and he definitely didn't like focus groups. The innovation process stayed fully inside Apple. As one book put it, the "lesson from Steve [is] don't listen to your customers." In order to create truly innovative devices, the thinking goes, Jobs had to reach beyond what customers could imagine. How else—I've often been asked—would Jobs have created the iPhone?

As a matter of fact, the iPhone is a perfect example of how Jobs included the customer.

THE IPHONE

Apple released its first cell phone in 2005, and it wasn't the iPhone. Developed in partnership with Motorola, the device was called the ROKR, and it was a flop. The user interface was clunky and confusing. The physical design had none of the sleek appeal of its predecessor, an impressively thin flip-phone called the RAZR. The music-storage feature that gave the ROKR its name was hamstrung by a limit of just a hundred songs. All of these shortcomings combined to create a disappointing customer experience and, unsurprisingly, the phone didn't sell well. Jobs was stung by the failure, feeling that Apple was blamed unfairly for Motorola's poor design, and he resolved that Apple would develop its own phone. Alone.

Cell phones at the time were poorly designed. Even the most basic features, like making a call or muting the ringer, were needlessly complicated. Voice mail—this is true—was intentionally designed to be hostile to customers. By slowing down the audio interface, carriers could extract more call minutes, and thus more revenue, from their customers. (Outraged by the flagrant abuse of customers, the *Times*' David Pogue launched a campaign called "Take Back the Beep," encouraging consumers to learn how to bypass lengthy voice prompts: "You don't have to sit there, waiting to leave your message, listening to a speech recorded by a third-grade teacher on Ambien.") Even getting a phone in the first place was a time-consuming, complex process requiring the customer to visit a physical store, compare different models, choose a plan and associated features, and then sign a detailed contract. The entire customer experience was painful and frustrating. Carriers, on the other hand, were comfortable with the arrangement, since the power resided squarely with them. Without any competition from a better device, there was no motivation to improve.

Steve Jobs very much had these issues in mind when Apple began work on the iPhone. As he told biographer Walter Isaacson: "We would sit around talking about how much we hated our phones. They were way too complicated. They had features nobody could figure out, including the address book. It was just Byzantine." Jobs knew that in a marketplace full of customer-hostile designs, a customer-friendly alternative could be a gigantic success.

It's worth noting what Jobs *didn't* say about the process. Here he was, sitting with some of the best designers in the world, with the opportunity to create a world-changing device. Did they start by thinking brilliant thoughts about radical new gadgets? Did they start with a blank whiteboard and brainstorm ideas about "the next big thing"? No. Jobs and his team began by taking the customers' perspective: Finding a contact was too hard. Sending a text message was clunky. Setting up a conference call was impossible. In other words, the iPhone was conceived from the very beginning to solve the problems in the customer experience of current smartphones. Stated a different way, the ultimate aim of the iPhone's design process, which informed every subsequent step of industrial and digital design, was to create benefits for the customer.

When Jobs finally unveiled the iPhone to the world in January 2007, he repeatedly framed the announcement in terms of how the design solved customer needs. Current smartphones, he said, are "not so smart and not so easy to use . . . it's amazing how hard it is to make calls on phones." The iPhone, in contrast, is "a leapfrog product that's way smarter than these phones and much easier to use." He then demonstrated that ease-of-use by making a call with the iPhone, then creating a three-way conference call. From the initial concept through the on-stage demo on launch day, the iPhone's development process was permeated by concern for the experience it would deliver to users.

The results were phenomenal. Over a million iPhones sold in the first three months alone, outselling the previous three months of *all* smartphones combined. Competitors were left reeling, wondering how to catch up. Long accustomed to extracting as much revenue as possible from their captive customers, manufacturers and carriers were now in the unfamiliar position of having to think about how to benefit customers. As *Wired* magazine put it not long after the iPhone launched, "Every manufacturer is racing to create a phone that consumers will love, instead of one that the carriers approve of."

Hold any iPhone in your hand and you have tangible proof that Steve Jobs did not ignore the customer. Quite the contrary. The devices *before* the iPhone were the ones ignoring, and opposing, the needs of customers. It was Jobs' focus on the customer experience that forced the industry to change.

"BUT STEVE JOBS NEVER ASKED."

A common response to the iPhone story goes like this: "Sure, the iPhone solved a customer need, but Jobs never asked customers what they wanted." After all, as the media repeatedly pointed out, Steve Jobs didn't like focus groups. So he and his team must have thought up the iPhone by themselves.

There's a common fallacy that the only way to include customers is to run a focus group and "ask people what they want." But that's obviously not true. There are many ways to go about doing research, as described in Part 2 of the book. (And Jobs was no stranger to customer research, as I'll point out below.) Despite his disdain for focus groups, Jobs did include the customer in his design process.

Again and again throughout his career, he demonstrated an intense concern for the experience that customers would have while using his products.

This began early on in his career. Walter Isaacson recounts the story of Jobs, at a design conference in 1983, describing the "desktop metaphor" of his new personal computer that would launch the following year. Jobs understood the potential of the windows-and-icons design (originally invented at Xerox PARC) to make computers much more widely accessible. "We have to make things intuitively obvious," he said, and since people were already familiar with real-world items like documents and folders, "we can leverage this experience people already have." Jobs, before the Mac was even launched, was describing it in terms of the user's experience. (Over twenty years later, the iPhone would "leverage the experience people have" of poorly designed smartphones.)

In the many articles about Jobs after his death, readers learned that he was a genius; he was hard to work with; he was a complicated character. But no one pointed out what I consider the real reason for his success: Steve Jobs bet the company on the customer experience. While other technology companies fretted about partnerships, or chipsets, or strengthening a monopoly, Jobs built a company culture around creating products that customers loved.

Jobs revealed the depth of this commitment at what might have been the riskiest moment in his career. In May 1997, months after returning to the company from an 11-year absence, Jobs held a "fireside chat" at Apple's annual Worldwide Developers Conference (WWDC). During the session, he fielded questions from developers who were understandably skeptical: Apple was a rudderless ship, near bankruptcy, with ineffective leadership and no definable strategy. One particularly hostile audience member asked Jobs "what you personally have been doing for the last seven years" and abruptly sat down. An audible boo rippled across the room. Video footage shows Jobs sitting quietly on his stool, head bowed, for almost fifteen seconds before launching into a brilliant ad-libbed speech.

Jobs said that to "effect change" one needs a "cohesive, larger vision" that can drive billions of dollars of sales. Then he revealed his vision to do just that:

> You've gotta start with the customer experience and work backwards to the technology. You can't start with the technology and try to figure out where you're going to try to sell it . . . As we have tried to come up with a strategy and a vision for Apple, it started with, "What incredible benefits can we give to the customer? Where can we take the customer?" not starting with, "Let's sit down with the engineers and figure out what awesome technology we have and then how are we gonna market that."

Jobs had just described his plan to save Apple. It's hard to imagine a clearer statement of intent: Apple would "start with the customer experience and work backwards," reversing the technology-centered approach that had brought the company to the brink of destruction. It was an incredibly bold move, telling an auditorium full of software developers—practically the last base of support Apple had—that the way forward would not be defined by technology. The company would now live or die based on whether it could create a good experience for its customers.

The results of this strategy are well known: the iMac, iPod, iTunes, iPhone, App Store, and iPad—for starters. What's not widely acknowledged is that these innovations, and the most dramatic turnaround in modern business history, were the direct result of the "customer experience" strategy that Jobs outlined at that 1997 event.

Furthermore, the WWDC was hardly the first indication that Jobs was obsessed with the user experience. John Sculley, Apple's CEO from 1983 to 1993, put it this way:

> At the beginning of the personal computer revolution, we both believed in beautiful design and Steve in particular felt that you had to begin design from the vantage point of the experience of the user.

> He always looked at things from the perspective of what was the user's experience going to be? But unlike a lot of

people in product marketing in those days, who would go
out and do consumer testing, asking people, "What did
they want?" Steve didn't believe in that.

Again we see that Jobs wasn't interested in asking people what they
wanted. Yet Jobs was clearly focused on the customer experience.
This was no tactical detail to be slotted in at the end of the product
development cycle; instead, Jobs considered—and stated explicitly!—that the customer experience was a *strategic* issue worthy of his
constant attention. (And lest it be said that Jobs never conducted any
customer research: Jobs would occasionally drop by the Apple Store
in Palo Alto to peek in. A former employee recalled how Jobs would
try to observe customers without causing a scene: "We would find
him hiding behind the bushes or around the corner outside, peering
inside to see what was going on.")

It is perfectly legitimate, then, to point out that customers
didn't design the iPhone. Steve Jobs, Jonathan Ive, and other Apple
designers did. But that doesn't mean that customers played no part.
To the contrary, Steve Jobs based his career, and his company, on
the idea that products should serve customers' needs—in his words,
creating "incredible benefits" for them. He managed to execute on
that idea by finding the best designers in the world and directing
them toward that task.

Late in his life, Jobs was asked at a press conference whether
his goal for Apple was to achieve greater market share. He took the
opportunity to make a larger point:

> I'll tell you what our goal is. Our goal is . . . to make
> products we are proud to sell and would recommend to
> our family and friends. I have to tell you, there's some
> stuff in our industry that we wouldn't be proud to ship,
> that we wouldn't be proud to recommend to our family and
> friends, and we can't do it. We just can't ship junk.

Here again Jobs revealed, as he did in 1997, what he was driving
Apple to accomplish. His aim wasn't primarily to create sleek gadgets
containing the latest technology, any more than it was to grab the
biggest market share. Those were secondary. Instead, Jobs had set

an even higher standard for Apple: benefiting the people who used its products.

It's absurd to try to generate great ideas without including customers in some way. But companies do it all the time, thinking they already know what customers want and so can avoid any contact with them. (The previous two chapters show the results of this approach.) Apple, in contrast, created great products precisely because Jobs valued the customer so highly. An exquisitely designed Apple device was not somehow above the customer, for the customer to aspire to. That has it exactly backwards. Jobs instead aspired to make products that were good enough to be worthy of the customer.

When Steve Jobs died, the world lost a singular leader, innovator, designer, and visionary. But the most important part of his legacy— his singular commitment to the customer experience—lives on in his company. (As of this writing, in early 2015, Apple is the world's largest company, by market capitalization, and just delivered the most profitable quarter of any company in history: $18 billion.)

If you want to emulate Jobs and the company he created, the lesson is simple: make decisions with customers included. Keep the customers' perspective in mind. Focus projects on benefiting the customer. And, of course, don't just ask people what they want. The next chapter describes what happened when Walmart made that mistake.

CHAPTER 3 SUMMARY

Steve Jobs' career is commonly offered as evidence that customers should be left out of the innovation process. This is a mistake. In this chapter I try to set the record straight that Jobs, in fact, demonstrated how to succeed by including the customer.

KEY POINTS

- Steve Jobs started with a passionate concern for the customer and "worked backwards" to the technology. (Contrast this with Google Wave, or the border fence project, which did the opposite.)
- Jobs focused the iPhone, from the very beginning, on creating a better customer experience. At the launch event itself, Jobs emphasized how the iPhone solved the long-standing frustrations of smartphone users.
- Anyone who wants to emulate Steve Jobs should focus on creating a good customer experience.

PART 2

THE METHOD

*"There's a customer-satisfaction questionnaire for you to fill out
and for us to not look at and immediately throw away."*

Bruce Eric Kaplan / The New Yorker Collection / www.cartoonbank.com

4

WHAT CUSTOMERS SAY

"The customers love it."

A few years ago, a friend of mine was shopping at a chain drug-store when something caught his attention. At every checkout counter was posted this sign:

How are we doing? Take our survey... give us a *9*
You have a chance to win $3,000.00!!

My friend didn't fill out the survey. I can't imagine that it generated much value for the store, since the sign explicitly asks for a high rating instead of a frank assessment of the customer experience. Practically begging customers to report good news, the sign is unlikely to elicit honest customer feedback. And then there is the mention of a lottery, suggesting that the winner of the cash prize might be drawn from responses with a high score.

As misconceived as the sign is, I can imagine how it could have come about. Perhaps company management launched an initiative to evaluate customer satisfaction across the network, rewarding top-scoring stores with a cash bonus, while managers of lagging stores would get penalized or fired. In such an environment, asking customers for a 9 seems innocuous enough. Who could blame a store manager for wanting to shore up his or her job security?

Granted, that's all hypothetical. But there was clearly some motivation for the store manager to seek artificially high numbers. Whatever the cause, this approach guaranteed that the company would get back skewed data, threatening the value of the entire exercise.

The drugstore survey is a good introduction to Part 2, which explores the strengths and weaknesses of various customer research methods. My message is simple: *The design of research affects the quality of the output.* Not all research is created equal. This chapter will show that research often fails to include meaningful customer input. Let's start with what may be the most popular research method in business today: the focus group.

ON FOCUS GROUPS

The focus group was invented by sociologist Robert Merton in the mid-20th century as a way to poll many people at once on their opinions of some product or idea. This decades-old research method is still widely popular and takes essentially the same form that it did when it was invented: a group of people sit in a room while a trained moderator peppers them with open-ended questions about their opinions and preferences on a given topic. Typically a group of researchers or executives watches from behind a mirrored one-way glass, and the session is videotaped for later review.

Focus groups are ubiquitous in research budgets today. Wherever the opinion of a group could help one choose from an available set of options, focus groups are likely to be found: rating alternative movie endings, weighing in on political campaign messaging, and anything in between. I want to emphasize that participants are sharing *opinions*, stated in a group environment, rather than demonstrating actual *behavior*, carried out in a real-life context. There are vast differences between those two types of data.

I'll grant that opinions can be helpful. If you have chunky spaghetti sauce in the pantry, in fact, you have indirectly benefited from focus groups. In a *New Yorker* article some years ago, Malcolm Gladwell explained why. A consumer products company, wanting to grow its sales of spaghetti sauce, commissioned a series of focus groups to discover what new type of sauce consumers might want. The research asked people for their opinion, after a taste test, of various aspects like sweetness and thickness. The results revealed a market opportunity for "chunky" sauces, which have since become very popular.

Since they can easily incorporate some kind of taste test, focus groups are a good match for food research. A few years ago, Domino's Pizza ran a nationally televised ad campaign showing focus group footage in which customers pronounced that its pizza tasted "like cardboard." This feedback, claimed the ad, prompted the company to reengineer its recipe and improve the taste of the pizza.

At Creative Good we've seen plenty of video footage of focus groups, as clients frequently ask us to watch the research they conducted before hiring us. These videos, rarely showing focus groups as effective as Domino's, have provided some memorable moments. One session in particular has always stayed with me.

A panel of respondents sits at a long table. In front of them stands the moderator, holding a cookie tin. He asks the respondents for their opinion of a certain feature on a website. When one person replies positively, the moderator opens the cookie tin and offers her a cookie. A second respondent gives a positive opinion and is handed the tin. But when a third raises her hand to comment that she might not use the feature, the moderator replies—direct quote here—"No cookie for you."

Of course, this moderator was hardly modeling the best way to facilitate a focus group. But even with a well-behaved moderator, the structure of the focus group has several inherent drawbacks:

1. As pointed out earlier, focus groups discover what people *think* (or say they think), rather than what they actually *do*. This emphasizes the *hypothetical* at the expense of the *actual*, a distinction that I will return to later in the chapter. Any team seeking to discover customers' unmet needs should instead observe real-life customer behavior. (Unmet needs are discussed more in Chapter 6.)

2. Focus groups observe multiple people at once, rather than individuals. This opens the research up to all sorts of unwanted influence from group dynamics. Talkative, dominant, or agreeable respondents can take attention away from people with dissenting opinions or introverted personalities.

3. The very structure of the group fails to approximate the real-world usage of most products and services. When research involves digital experiences, like websites and apps, this becomes particularly problematic. It would make no sense, for example, to ask a group of people to call out their reactions to a mobile app: in what real-life situation does someone use the same iPad simultaneously with a dozen other people?

4. Organizational politics, on the client side, can influence the research. In the "no cookie" example above, the moderator almost certainly had some motivation to steer the outcome toward a desired result. The design of focus groups unfortunately leaves them susceptible to this type of influence, since the moderator must actively guide the session.

All four of these drawbacks were visible in a focus group that I participated in several years ago. A major car manufacturer was offering test drives of their new models as an incentive to participate. Interested in taking a test drive and learning how this well-known company conducted its research, I signed up.

I was led, with about a dozen other people, into a meeting room with several rows of seats, arranged classroom-style. Standing at the front of the room was the moderator, whom I'll call Chad. After introducing himself, Chad asked his first question: "Can anyone tell me what you'd like to see online from a car company?" No one answered, leaving an awkward silence in the room. Chad smiled. "Really? No one has ideas? OK, well, if you were going to shop for a car online, what would you do?" After a few moments one of the attendees, a middle-aged man, tentatively raised a hand and said, "I'd probably want to find out what kinds of cars were available, and what their features were." Chad beamed as he walked over to stand in front of the man. "Great, great," Chad said, "find out their features. OK, now can you say *how* you'd like to see those features? Any particular way?" The man shrugged.

Undeterred, Chad returned to the front of the room and addressed the group. "Can anyone think of some way they'd like to get car info online? I want you to think big." He looked from face to face. No one spoke up. "Don't worry about how it would get done, just think really *big.*" Finally, a voice from the back of the room: "I'd use something simple, with some text and links, just showing a list of the cars." Chad looked back at the speaker. "Hmm," he said, noticeably less enthused. "OK, but really, I want everyone to think really big about this: what would be a really cool way to learn about these cars online? What feature would make that possible?"

Now a third respondent spoke up, tentatively: "Maybe . . . video?" Chad's face lit up as though he had won a small sweepstakes. "Yes! Video! Exactly." The respondent looked quizzical, as Chad seemed much more excited about the idea than he was. "OK," Chad asked the group while bouncing on his toes, "let's talk about this idea of video. How might we design a website, using *video*, to show off the cars?" In the back of the room, the second respondent raised his hand again. "I'm not sure I'd want video. It takes too long to load. What about just getting information in a format that would load faster?"

Chad appeared to fight back irritation. "Maybe, but let's just follow up on this really intriguing idea about video. Let me ask again: who has some ideas about a website featuring car videos?" The session continued in this manner. Chad kept begging for blue-sky ideas relating to video, while the respondents mostly sat back in their chairs, watching the clock for the moment they'd be released to the test drive.

By telling this story, I'm not suggesting that focus groups should never be run. After all, they can be very effective in polling multiple people for their opinions or preferences (and for bringing chunky spaghetti sauce into the world). But there's a risk. Apart from the hazards of a poorly trained (or overly coached) moderator, focus groups have the inherent drawback that they show what customers *say* rather than what they *do*. Surveys have the same weakness, and as shown in the next case study, that can cause all sorts of trouble.

THE WALMART SURVEYS

A few years ago, before the Great Recession arrived, Target was enjoying an uptick in sales. American shoppers, showing their newfound interest in "upmarket" brands, flocked to Target stores to browse clean, well-lit aisles displaying curated selections of products, some created by celebrity designers. For a discount retailer, it was a surprisingly pleasant shopping experience. This was in contrast to Target's chief competitor, Walmart, where customers shopped in warehouse-like spaces, under dim lighting, with aisles crammed with products.

Aisles at Walmart. (©2014 Angela Smith. All rights reserved.)

The no-frills approach had never been a problem for Walmart. To the contrary, Sam Walton's fanatical devotion to cost-cutting (dim lighting was cheaper!) had been instrumental to the company's success. Customers came to Walmart not for its ambience or elegant taste but for two reasons: a wide selection of products and low prices. This had been Walmart's approach for decades, and it was well known to every executive in the company. Yet some executives were beginning to have doubts.

The problem was Target. Sales data showed that more and more affluent customers were abandoning Walmart to shop there. Perhaps, some executives thought, it might be time for Walmart to reconsider its strategy. Maybe wide selection and low prices weren't enough for some customers. If so, Walmart might be able to win them back if the stores could improve their chaotic and cluttered look.

There was data supporting this thinking. Recent in-store surveys reported that customers, especially women, didn't like the clutter in the aisles, the disorganization of the stores, and the general hassle of shopping there. These customers said that they wanted a cleaner, more pleasant experience. The *Pittsburgh Post-Gazette* reported it this way:

> [Walmart] not long ago discovered many of its paying clientele—a female-dominated group that has spent billions at its stores and helped it become the world's largest retailer—didn't like some of its most distinctive features. In surveys, customers said . . . they wanted the [stores] to be faster, friendlier and cleaner.

The survey data offered a compelling answer to the competitive challenge from Target. Customers said they wanted Walmart to be cleaner and better designed. Correspondingly, sales data showed that customers were abandoning Walmart for the rival who was—guess what—cleaner and better designed. How much more obvious could customers make it?

Walmart leadership decided to act. In short order, Walmart launched a massive, company-wide initiative to "improve the customer shopping experience" called Project Impact. The man appointed to lead the entire effort was chief merchandising officer John Fleming, who had been hired as chief marketing officer just a few years earlier. One might wonder why a relative newcomer to Walmart—and a marketer at that—would oversee such an important change to the company's merchandising strategy. Fleming apparently had the exact experience that Walmart wanted, having come to the company after spending almost twenty years at another retailer, known for its upscale shopping experience. That company was Target.

Walmart began rolling out redesigned stores in early 2009. Aisles were de-cluttered and products were displayed more attractively. Shelves were less tall, "end caps" (promotional displays at either end of an aisle) were removed, and inventory in "Action Alley," the main thoroughfare through the center of the store, was pruned enough to provide, in the words of one executive, "clear sight lines" throughout the store. All of these changes were significant departures from Sam Walton's merchandising strategy: "Stack 'em high, watch 'em fly." Now with fewer products on sale, the stacks were a lot less high.

Customers walking into redesigned stores immediately noticed the change. Not only were there clear aisles and less clutter, but by some estimates, 15% of the store inventory had vanished. Recall that Walmart's long-standing strategy had two components: low prices and a wide variety of brands. Now, in many cases, customers' favorite brands were gone. This was especially problematic in the grocery aisles. If a customer couldn't find a brand she was loyal to—a certain mayonnaise, for example—she might leave Walmart to pick it up at a competing grocery chain. Once in the other store, she'd note the wide product selection and decide to shop there from then on. Project Impact had cleared a wide, unobstructed path for more customers to abandon Walmart.

In October 2009, just a few months into Project Impact, *Retailer Daily* reported the results so far. It was not the result Walmart wanted. Not only had Project Impact failed to capture Target's customers, but "Target appears to be gaining some of Walmart's expansive market share." What's more, Walmart had reported negative quarterly growth for the previous year or so, while Target had reported *positive* growth in nearly every month during that time. Despite Walmart's costly attempt to lure away Target's customers, Target's numbers were going *up*—and during a recession, when most other retailers were being hit hard. This was a disastrous outcome for Walmart.

Around that time, Walmart's investors got a chance to ask for an explanation. Mike Duke, who had become CEO of Walmart soon after Project Impact was launched, fielded questions at a Goldman Sachs retail conference. At one point Duke was asked about "comp sales"—the change in sales numbers, in a given store, from one year to the next. Duke attempted to deflect the question:

> You do measure comp sales, but you really measure what
> does the customer think, and those measures are very
> positive . . . Many of you would have been in stores where
> you might not see the amount of product in the aisles, for
> example. That is part of the strategy. And the customers
> love it.

Duke is saying, essentially, let's not dwell on unpleasant sales
figures—what's really important is that customers *say* they love
the new stores. That same week, *Fortune* magazine quoted another
Walmart executive with a different take. He gave a two-sentence case
study of Project Impact: "What happened was, shoppers said, 'We
love clean aisles.' But they stopped shopping there." Customers' positive survey responses had not translated into positive sales figures.
This is one of the most important concepts in the book, so I'll state
it as clearly as I can: *There's a big difference between what customers say
and what they do.*

Walmart's surveys asked customers to *say* whether they would
prefer cleaner, less cluttered stores. The company never tried to find
out whether customers would *do* anything different—that is, buy
more stuff—in such an environment. Surveys ask people to *say* what
they want, just as focus groups ask respondents to state their opinions. These are hypothetical statements, very different from observations of actual customer behavior. Walmart could have gained much
more insight from observing customers.

If Walmart had asked Creative Good for help on this strategic
decision, my team would have gone to the stores to spend time with
customers. We would have watched them shop, then asked them
(non-leading) follow-up questions to clarify our understanding of
their experience. Those direct observations, combined with a quantitative analysis of in-store sales data, would have revealed the enduring
importance of Walmart's wide selection and low prices. Without ever
asking a customer, "Do you want uncluttered aisles?", this process
could have provided a factual basis to avoid, or at least modify,
Project Impact.

Unfortunately, Walmart focused on the hypothetical—what

customers said—and suffered the result. Not long after the CEO's talk with investors, the entire Project Impact strategy was quietly rolled back. Action Alley began to fill back up with cluttered displays, and formerly stocked products and brands returned to the shelves. John Fleming, the former Target executive who led Project Impact, left Walmart within a year. The company clearly wanted to move on from the fiasco. The once high-profile initiative had been highlighted in Walmart's 2009 and 2010 annual reports but didn't get a single mention in the 2011 annual report.

The cost of Project Impact was not as easy to forget. Hundreds of millions of dollars had gone into remodeling the stores, followed by the considerable expense of returning them to their original state. And that wasn't the worst of it. Recall that in late 2009, CEO Mike Duke had sidestepped a question about troubling sales data, saying instead that "customers love it." A little over a year later, Walmart released an earnings report showing that comp sales—the very metric Duke had avoided talking about—had declined, every quarter, for seven quarters in a row. There was no escaping the fact that Walmart had gotten hammered.

It's hard to imagine Sam Walton presiding over such a botched process. For a man who delighted in walking through stores and chatting up shoppers and employees, it would have been inconceivable to adopt a new strategic direction, at great expense, without a firm understanding of the customer. Yet that is just what Walmart did.

Walmart executives might have avoided the entire mess with a bit of wisdom by Sam Walton: "The secret of successful retailing is to give your customers what they want." Project Impact failed, to put it bluntly, because it wasn't what customers wanted. Yes, customers said on surveys that they wanted clear aisles and decluttered stores. But that's not what Sam Walton meant. Here is a corollary to the principle above: What customers *say* they want is often different from what they *actually* want.

WORDS VS. BEHAVIOR

Words are very different from behavior. In their book *Practical Wisdom*, Barry Schwartz and Kenneth Sharpe give a clue why. Citing multiple studies revealing a mismatch between respondents' words and behavior, Schwartz and Sharpe conclude that "the features of an . . . experience that are most important to us may not be easy to verbalize, and the features that are easy to verbalize may not be that important." In other words, what people say may just be what's easiest to say.

The Walmart case is proof of how dangerous it is to base a strategy on what customers say. Why, then, do companies choose hypothetical data from surveys and focus groups, when actual data from direct customer observation would be so much more valuable? I suspect that inertia often plays a part—as in, "this is what we've always done." Mention customer research and many people immediately think of focus groups or surveys. The very popularity of these methods makes them easier to choose.

In Walmart's case, observational research would have been far more valuable. But—here's the rub—it also would have been more difficult. Walmart executives who were so intent on beating Target probably would not have liked hearing that their approach was the wrong one. Beyond any concerns of ego, this finding would have revealed to executives that they needed to spend more time crafting their strategy. Although unpleasant to hear, this insight could have saved Walmart hundreds of millions of dollars. The surveys had made it too easy to choose the wrong decision.

Including the customer is hard work. Any team genuinely seeking customer insight will discover that there are no shortcuts. This doesn't prevent some companies from trying to find one—which presents a perfect opportunity for a method that, when misused, appears to generate customer insight while not involving customers at all. This is the method of "personas," and it requires some explanation.

ABOUT PERSONAS

Whether practiced well or not, personas always involve the creation of made-up customers. For example, a car company might create a persona representing a new mom who values safety above all else, and a persona of a middle-aged executive who wants enough trunk space to hold his golf clubs. Rallying the team around these two personas can help guide the design process. (For instance, the team would know not to design a sports car with a small trunk, since that would satisfy neither persona.)

At first glance, this may appear to be nothing more than customer segmentation. For example, the car company might just as easily identify "young mothers" and "middle-aged executives who play golf" as customer segments to serve. But personas go much further than this, requiring each fictional character to be given a name, a picture (usually taken from a stock photo database), and a whole host of specific details about their life: where they went to school, how many kids they have, their TV-watching habits, and so on.

So instead of "young mothers" we'd have Connie. She is twenty-eight, lives in Grand Rapids, originally born in Minneapolis. Has one three-year-old son and a newborn daughter. She used to work as a home health aid, but now stays home with the kids and hopes to someday go back to school for a nursing degree. She and her husband (married for five years) root for the Chicago Bears but haven't watched many games since the second child came. Treats herself to Starbucks once a week. Drives a 2012 Camry. And so on.

Personas are supposed to encourage the team to consider how these fictive people would, hypothetically, feel about various product decisions. This might seem to raise the team's general awareness about customers. But personas have the obvious shortcoming that *these people don't exist*. No matter how many details one invents about a fictitious character, doing so generates no insight about how actual people would use a product. Personas invented out of thin air are the embodiment of a team's own internal assumptions and beliefs.

But personas don't have to be created out of thin air. When based on previous customer research, personas can serve as a helpful summary of what was learned from observing actual, real-life people. Given that it would bring a dramatic improvement to the accuracy of personas, one might expect that actual customer research would be strongly and repeatedly recommended by the proponents of the method. Unfortunately, that's not always the case.

For example, the 2010 book *The Essential Persona Lifecycle* briefly mentions customer observation as one of several possible data sources to guide persona creation. But it's optional. If the team already has enough "embedded knowledge" about customers—that is, if the team is confident it already knows what customers want—there's no need to run actual research. "Most businesses," the authors write, "are not rocket science."

Given the literature's lack of emphasis on including real customers in the process, it's no surprise that personas today are often created without any direct customer observation. The time it takes to invent exhaustive fictional details of characters' lives, it seems, leaves little time to get to know actual customers. In fact, I've encountered teams that have spent months concocting their personas before moving on to subsequent project phases.

When created in the absence of actual customers, personas end up prioritizing the hypothetical over the actual, and fiction over fact. My team once witnessed this first-hand while running research for a client that had created personas—without prior customer research— before hiring Creative Good. In one memorable research session, as everyone watched a user struggle helplessly with the client's app, one of the observing executives declared that the customer being observed was "wrong." The executive explained that she had helped create the persona named "Steve," and "Steve would never do that." Given a choice between observing what was happening in front of her and believing her own fictional construct, she vehemently chose the latter. The experience of observing real people can be a shock to executives who are accustomed to paying attention only to fictional characters they invented out of whole cloth.

The danger of personas, when misused in this way, is that they can generate false confidence in faulty conclusions. By filling invented personas with dozens of fictional details, it may feel like we know these people and thus can make decisions on their behalf. This irrational line of thought is a known psychological phenomenon. In his outstanding book *Thinking, Fast and Slow*, Nobel laureate Daniel Kahneman describes the act of "jumping to conclusions on the basis of limited evidence." This was a key factor in Walmart's mistake, and it's central to personas. He writes:

> The confidence that individuals have in their beliefs depends mostly on the quality of the story they can tell about what they see, even if they see little. We often fail to allow for the possibility that evidence that should be critical to our judgment is missing.

In other words, if personas are drawn richly enough, they can induce us to draw conclusions about the characters, and make decisions on their behalf, as though we knew them in real life. As Kahneman points out, the "quality of the story" can cause us to overlook that important data is missing. Once you get to know your imaginary friends well enough, it's easy to conclude that you don't need to listen to real-life people.

And this is precisely why personas can be a misguided investment, if they don't involve direct customer research beforehand. Every hour spent considering what an imaginary person "would" want from a product, or how they "would" react to a decision, could be spent observing how actual people *do* react, and what they *do* want. Relying on fictional people to guide a decision is a lot like ignoring customers altogether, except that it costs more.

I'm hardly the only person opposed to faulty personas. One of the most vocal critics of their misuse is Alan Cooper, the inventor of personas. His 1999 book *The Inmates Are Running the Asylum* was the first to describe how and why personas can be used effectively, though Cooper told me in an interview that his method has been widely misinterpreted since then:

> What's happened is, some people have said, 'Oh personas, I get it, this is really cool,' and then they've used them wrong. They've used them as a bludgeon to get their

own way and to express their own desires rather than expressing the desires of the user. You know, 'We really want to put in this feature where you push this button and this screen comes up. So what we need is a persona that needs to push this button to get this screen.'

Cooper emphasized the importance of directly observing users, to discover their goals (he has been advocating for "goal-directed design" for decades), and "goals are expressed through personas." I told Cooper that I've encountered companies that have spent months concocting personas without any customer research beforehand. Cooper was adamant:

> Those are not personas. You can't call those personas. I don't know what they are. If you don't do patient, humble observation, I don't care what kind of personas you create. It doesn't matter. You're just cooking up stuff in your head.

I'm occasionally asked by Creative Good clients to create personas. I'm happy to agree to do so, on the condition that the client allows us to first run customer research, with actual people, in listening labs. (More on that in Chapter 7.) Once we have analyzed the research results, we produce a list of the major distinctions between the various customer types, and what their goals are. In this way, we're able to provide the benefits of personas without ever relying on hypothetical data. Like any other method, personas can be valuable if customers are included in the process.

Fortunately, there are research methods that are more commonly practiced to include direct customer observation. I will cover these types of research in the following three chapters. Chapter 5 will explore task-based usability, which focuses on the tactical improvement of a tool. (As we'll see, there are historical reasons why it works this way.) Then Chapter 6 will explore the idea of "unmet needs" and show how direct customer observation is so successful in discovering them. Finally, Chapter 7 will describe listening labs, a research method pioneered by Creative Good that helps companies include the customer by directly observing actual people.

CHAPTER 4 SUMMARY

Part 1 of the book describes the importance of including the customer. Part 2, starting with this chapter, explores the various ways of doing that.

KEY POINTS

- There's a difference between what customers *say* and what they *do*.

- Popular research methods like focus groups and surveys tend to generate data that is hypothetical (what customers say) rather than actual (what they do).

- Walmart's expensive misstep, using survey data to justify a strategic decision, was summarized this way: "Shoppers said, 'We love clean aisles.' But they stopped shopping there."

- Personas, unless based on prior customer research, can tempt a team to make decisions based purely on hypothetical data (what fictional people "would" want).

5

USERS AND TASKS

"They read their altimeter wrong."

Imagine you've been given the chance to test-drive a new model car. Perhaps you're an automotive journalist, or maybe you just sat through a focus group, as described in the previous chapter. Someone hands you the keys, you walk out to the parking lot, sit down in the driver's seat, start the engine, and begin driving. A few minutes into the drive, you have to pull over. Moments later you get back on the road, but then you have to pull over again. What would you guess is going on?

This actually happened when reviewers from *Popular Mechanics* faced a recurring problem during their test drive of the 2013 Ford Fusion. "We repeatedly had to pull over," they wrote of the incident. The issue, as it turns out, lay in the "center stack," the console that allows the driver and passenger to tune the radio, control the air conditioning, and so on. Most consoles have buttons and knobs big enough for a driver to find and manipulate without looking away from the road. The 2013 Ford Fusion was different: its design had replaced the traditional layout with a futuristic, minimalist interface centered around a touchscreen. As the *Popular Mechanics* review put it, "the touchscreen's buttons are too few, too small, and too confusing to navigate." The only safe way for a driver to use the features was to pull over.

The touchscreen, part of a high-tech suite of features called MyFord Touch, was officially launched in January 2010 at the Consumer Electronics Show (CES), an annual conference and trade show featuring the latest gadgetry and gee-whiz features from the electronics industry. The system allowed customers to control temperature, music, and much more with the computerized interface; the traditional buttons and knobs for these features were largely absent. A Ford executive promised that the new system would "help consumers fall in love with their vehicles again." Offering its review on the day of the launch, technology blog Engadget called MyFord Touch "the dashboard of the future" and deemed it "intuitive and easy to use." Like the initial reviews of Google Wave, there was no mention of anyone using the product outside of the launch event.

Once Ford began rolling out the new system to its cars, trucks, and SUVs, a very different reaction surfaced. *Popular Mechanics* was not alone in noting the deeply flawed design. Autoguide.com called the system "an unfortunate mess," citing the difficulty of using the maps feature. (Presumably they didn't try it at sixty miles an hour.) And then there was *Consumer Reports*:

> The MyTouch controls give a new meaning to the word "unfriendly." Most of the controls have lost their simple knobs and have been replaced with touch-sensitive buttons that give no tactile feedback. The system also has busy touch screens that force you to take your eyes off the road too much. All-in-all, it's an aggravating design.

In 2012 Ford released a software update, but it didn't fix the problem. *Consumer Reports* published a litany of complaints about the new system, concluding that "we wouldn't recommend dealing with the frustrations of MyFord Touch even to an adversary."

MyFord Touch also included a voice-recognition system that promised to allow drivers access to functions without taking their eyes off the road. Even when tested in ideal conditions, without other passengers talking, the system was unreliable and did not make up for the flaws in the touchscreen. The plain fact was that Ford had taken away something that its customers had relied on. "The days of reaching for a knob or preset button without looking are gone," *Consumer Reports* lamented. (News broke in early 2014 that Ford was abandoning the voice-recognition system, developed by Microsoft, and replacing it with new software.)

MyFord Touch.

Shown above is MyFord Touch in a 2014 Ford Flex. Below the problematic touchscreen are the physical controls for the radio and temperature. Important features like "Seek" and "My Temp" have no visible buttons, forcing users to poke at the vertical surface of the dashboard and hope that they land on the touch-sensitive area. (Pushing the chrome on either side of the knobs does nothing; it's purely decorative.) I asked the owner what he thinks of MyFord Touch, now that he's driven the car for over a year. "I was just complaining about these controls to a friend yesterday," he told me. "I can't stand them."

Customers have been vocal in their disappointment with MyFord Touch. YouTube videos demonstrating the system are littered with complaints from owners, calling it "a wreck," "a disaster," as well as some unprintable names. A more rigorous study of customer complaints came from J.D. Power's annual Initial Quality Study, ranking automotive brands by the number of problems reported by customers. Ford, known for its reliability, had previously been ranked among the best. The year before MyFord Touch appeared, Ford ranked 5th out of about 30 brands. In 2011 it fell to 23rd. The reason for the drop, said J.D. Power, was customer complaints about MyFord Touch. (It didn't end there. In 2012 Ford fell to 27th, and then in 2013, after the touchscreen update, Ford fell to 28th out of 34 brands—prompting the *Detroit Free Press* to ask whether MyFord Touch might be "just too complicated.")

The key question is how Ford managed to commit such an obvious error. Founded in 1903, Ford Motor Company had dealt with technological change before. What caused the company to lose its focus on quality in 2010? More specifically, why did Ford remove something that drivers wanted, and replace it with a product that threatened their safety?

Some clues are available in a conference presentation given by two members of the MyFord Touch design team shortly after the system launched. The presenters describe their innovation process, which involved weeks of brainstorming in seclusion—"we literally camped out and nobody saw us for many months"—followed by the rapid construction of a prototype, after which customers were brought in to go through "predefined tasks." (More on these later in the chapter.)

The result was a sleek, futuristic design that art-school designers might appreciate aesthetically, but that ignored the needs of the people who would actually use the system.

DILBERT ©2013 *Scott Adams. Used by permission of UNIVERSAL UCLICK. All rights reserved.*

It may seem strange that such a rigorous design process, including some amount of user research, would yield a product with a fundamental design flaw. Yet it is very common. When a design process doesn't take users' needs into account, the result is bound to be problematic. As Ford showed, making even small changes to a few buttons can affect the driver's overall performance with the vehicle. This is not a new insight. As we'll see, some of the earliest user interfaces suffered from a remarkably similar problem.

WHY THE B-17S KEPT CRASHING

In 1943, the U.S. Army Air Forces faced a peculiar problem: B-17 bombers kept crashing in the last few seconds of their flights. After surviving the perils of a dangerous mission, evading enemy fighters and dodging anti-aircraft flak along the way, the bombers would return to base, where the incident would occur. Just after the plane's wheels touched down on the runway, the pilot would reach forward and retract the landing gear, causing the plane to slam into the tarmac at full speed.

These incidents were documented as pilot error, but the cause remained a mystery. Why would a highly skilled pilot make such a basic mistake? And why did pilots of some planes, but not others, do it? (B-17s, B-25s, P-47s, and C-46s all had runway crashes, while C-47s seemed immune.) Was it a lack of training? Fatigue from a long and stressful flight? The Army—which poured massive resources into hiring and training capable pilots who wouldn't make such mistakes—needed to determine what was going on.

The task went to Lieutenant Alphonse Chapanis, a 25-year-old who had just completed a PhD in psychology from Yale. Though young and inexperienced—he had joined the Army a few months before—Chapanis turned out to be an excellent choice, as he quickly found what was causing the crashes. It's true that pilots were retracting the landing gear on the runway, but that was merely a symptom of an underlying problem.

Chapanis's key insight was that the crashes were not due to pilot error. Nor were the crashes due to poor training, a lack of skill, or any other deficiency of the pilot. Instead, the problem was clearly visible on the instrument panel. The switch controlling the landing gear was located adjacent to a nearly identical switch that operated the flaps. When the plane's wheels touched down, and the pilot reached forward to retract the flaps, it was all too easy to select the wrong switch.

Having identified the problem, Chapanis developed a solution that was inexpensive, easy to install, and surprisingly simple: he differentiated the two switches. On the landing gear switch he added a small rubber handle in the shape of a tire, while on the flaps switch he put a wedge-shaped handle. The shape and feel made the mapping easy to remember: tires for landing, wedge for flaps. B-17s and other planes were quickly outfitted with these handles, and the runway crashes stopped almost immediately. It was such an effective solution, in fact, that many planes today still feature some version of those switch handles. (And as for the C-47, the reason it didn't suffer runway crashes was that its landing gear and flap switches were not adjacent.)

5. Landing Gear Switch
6. Wing Flap Switch

B-17 control panel. (B-17 Pilot Training Manual for the Flying Fortress)

The cockpit of a World War II bomber contained dozens of switches, levers, handles, throttles, buttons, locks, and other controls, as well as an instrument panel of altitude, airspeed, fuel levels, compass, and other indicators—not to mention the audio interface of alarms and radio communications. This density of data, and this degree of interactive complexity, had never been seen before: not in mechanical control systems, not even in previous airplanes. What's more, there was a huge penalty for error. A single button pressed by mistake, or a second too late, could be catastrophic. The Army's initial response to this was to recruit the smartest, most psychologically sound candidates it could find, then train them rigorously to minimize the incidence of pilot error.

Chapanis showed that this approach was insufficient. By pointing out the design flaw of the adjacent switches, he revealed that it was the plane, not the pilot, that needed to change. Specifically, the improvement would have to occur in the thin layer mediating the pilot's connection to the plane's vast array of capabilities. This layer was something new: it wasn't a physical tool, nor a tool controlling other tools as in a control system, but something more complex, more abstract, more cognitive. It was a user interface.

And the interface could be improved. Take a massive plane, and the thousands of hours (and millions of dollars) of engineering that went into it, and the highly trained crew operating it, and now layer in a little arrangement of switches and levers in the cockpit. Outcome: the plane crashes. Now take the same plane but glue a two-inch-wide toy tire onto one of the switches: the plane survives! Small improvements in an interface could make the difference between disaster and success. And the way to identify those improvements was to take the user's perspective.

THE "PILOT ERROR" REPORTS

Chapanis wasn't alone in exploring this topic. In 1947, the newly formed U.S. Air Force published groundbreaking research by Dr. Paul Fitts and Captain R. E. Jones, who had studied hundreds of wartime mishaps that were designated "pilot errors." Many incidents had something to do with pilots misreading the flight instruments in the cockpit. Fitts and Jones repeatedly point out, in two reports on the topic, that pilots were usually not to blame. Instead, the problem lay squarely in the interface. One report sums it up this way: "It should be possible to eliminate a large proportion of so-called 'pilot-error' accidents by designing equipment in accordance with human requirements."

The reports are fascinating, if occasionally macabre. Poor design and layout of instrument panels directly contributed to hundreds of life-threatening circumstances. The numbers are conservative, since the data came only from pilots who survived their incidents. As one put it, "Pilots are pushing up plenty of daisies today because they read their altimeter wrong."

The altimeter design was to blame for a number of accidents, as it was dangerously easy for pilots to confuse vastly different readings. One pilot described his experience this way:

> In setting the altimeter of a B-17 to field elevation, I once made an error of 1,000 feet. Instead of setting the altimeter at plus 800, I set it at minus 200 feet. In this position, the large pointer also points to the 800 foot position.

Other instruments in the cockpit were also problematic. Several incidents resulted from the design of the directional gyro—essentially the plane's compass—which displayed only the first two digits of the three-digit heading: "1" stood for 10, "18" stood for 180. Pilots were trained to mentally add a zero when they read the heading, but in stressful moments, some forgot that step. In such a case, a pilot intending to fly toward 20 would mistakenly steer toward the "20" on the directional gyro. Doing so would fly the plane at 200—exactly opposite the intended direction. During combat it could be a fatal mistake.

As notable as the findings were, what's perhaps more distinctive is the research method the authors used. In a surprisingly open, non-directed fashion, interviewers asked pilots to describe their experiences in the cockpit when the errors occurred. The focus was getting the pilots' stories, without judgement or leading questions. This allowed pilots to open up and accurately relate their experience in the cockpit. Had military brass dictated a different approach—for example, launching an investigation into pilot mistakes—the cockpit design problems might never have surfaced. Instead, by keeping an open mind and allowing the pilots to share freely, the researchers allowed the truth to emerge from the conversations. (As we'll see, these free-flowing interviews were very different from the task-oriented methods that were developed a few years later.)

Fitts and Jones were also unusual in taking an interest in everyday pilots, who were typically not asked for design input. One aviation historian explained that "the majority of the pilots whose opinions were sought on the layout and equipment of a new cockpit were very experienced aviators." Although it might seem that expert pilots would give helpful feedback, this typically wasn't the case. Aviation psychologist Stanley Roscoe, a contemporary of Fitts and Jones, noted that when "veteran pilots were consulted, each tended to go along with existing precedent and resist change." This left cockpit design decisions to be made "almost by default." The vast majority of pilots had never been given a voice until the Fitts and Jones research.

The 1947 reports had a lasting influence well beyond the design of cockpits. While Chapanis's B-17 project revealed the supreme importance of a well-designed interface, Fitts and Jones showed the role that users themselves could play in the interface design process. No longer did the design of switches and buttons have to be evaluated only by expert pilots who would "resist change." Now interface design could include the perspective of everyday users: the very people who could point out what needed to improve, indeed the very people whose lives depended on that design.

It is hard to overstate the importance of these early forays into user research and interface design. These days, as we interact with countless devices, apps, and sites on a regular basis, we take for granted the importance of a well-designed interface. And companies spend giant sums to recruit and hire teams of user experience researchers and interaction designers. This widespread awareness of, and investment in, interface design got its start in the 1940s. In hindsight it's obvious that interface design was a life-or-death issue in the bombers' instrument panels—yet it took the pioneering work of Chapanis, Fitts, and Jones to point out these fundamental ideas:

- There's such a thing as a user interface. It's not quite a tool, but rather a thin layer separating the user from (and giving the user leverage over) the tool.
- If users make mistakes while using the interface, it's probably the fault of the interface design, not the user.
- The way to discover improvements is to listen to everyday users—not expert insiders—as they describe their experience with the interface.
- Improving an interface has real-world outcomes, like accidents prevented and lives saved.

Every student of interaction design and user experience should know the work of Chapanis, Fitts, and Jones—if only because the lessons of their work are even more broadly applicable and important today.

Despite their tremendous contributions, Fitts and Jones didn't permanently correct the problems in cockpit interface design. Accidents still occur today due to problems remarkably similar to those documented in the 1940s. One such incident occurred in 2004, when an F-16 fighter jet, on a training mission from its base in Maryland, accidentally machine-gunned a middle school in New Jersey. (Luckily, this took place at night, and no one was harmed.) An investigation into the accident revealed that the same trigger on the F-16's joystick controlled both a targeting system and the gun. The pilot squeezed the trigger a little too hard and strafed the school. In the aftermath of the accident, the Air Force released an incident report listing the causes of the mishap. A "poorly designed . . . interface" is included in the list, but it appears second. The first item is "pilot error."

One reason Fitts and Jones' methods weren't more fully adopted was due to what happened in the years after their reports were published. It explains a lot about how user research is often practiced today.

THE BIRTH OF USABILITY

"Man is quite a different component from an electron tube." This vivid observation appears in a 1957 paper, published by the Naval Research

Laboratory, comparing and contrasting human beings with machine parts. The authors write that when designing systems, one should take into account the "general characteristics of man as a system component," including "capability for data sensing," "capability for data processing," and others. Such language may sound a little strange today, but it wasn't out of place in America's postwar industrial society. In a time of mass marketing, cookie-cutter houses, and "the man in the gray flannel suit," reliability and conformity were familiar and desirable qualities. Today's conception of customers—individualistic, networked, and in control—would have been quite foreign.

User research in the 1950s no longer resembled the informal, collegial interviews of Fitts and Jones but instead reflected the mechanization of the time. Pilots were considered components— an Air Force report around this time refers to them as "personnel subsystems"—and like any other part in the system, they needed testing. (An amusing counterpoint in the Naval Research Laboratory paper comes from none other than Alphonse Chapanis: "Call a man a machine if you want to, but don't underestimate him when you come to do experiments on him. He's a nonlinear machine.") While Fitts and Jones had focused attention on the experience of the human being piloting the plane, now the *tasks* were the focal point of user research. This thinking was codified by 1965, when an Air Force report documented "Task-Analysis of Procedures" and other task-based processes as commonly used research methods. Task-based usability had arrived.

In task-based usability, a researcher gives the user a list of prewritten tasks, then records whether the user completes them successfully. (This is the metric of "task success," which can be accompanied by other measurements like time taken, number of actions required, and so on.) Consistent with the academic and military context in which it originated, the method lacks concern for larger business-related issues like strategy or profitability. Nevertheless, task-based usability became a mainstay of user research in the business world and is still in use today—indeed, as noted earlier, it was used during the MyFord Touch project.

Usability has shown remarkable longevity, given the degree to which user interfaces have changed since the 1950s. With the arrival of the PC in the 1980s, the web in the 1990s, and mobile devices in the 2000s, millions—now billions—of people have interacted with user interfaces. Yet still to this day, many usability researchers will assign a respondent a set of prewritten tasks and then measure his or her task success—as though the user were an Air Force pilot in 1955. As one would expect, there are some shortcomings to the method.

DRAWBACKS OF USABILITY RESEARCH

The main drawback to task-based usability testing is that the tasks are all determined by the researchers beforehand. This means users may be asked to perform tasks that have no relevance to them, which then calls into question the significance of the test results. (As discussed in Chapter 7, it's far better to observe users doing the things they would normally do outside a research setting.) Prewritten tasks might be appropriate when testing pilots' abilities to go through certain well-defined procedures, but that's not a useful model for today's users, who exercise far more autonomy in their customer experiences.

Even if the prewritten tasks happen to be relevant to users, there's another issue: the insights gained from the usability test are limited by those tasks. This can prevent researchers from seeing other, more important insights outside that scope. For example, a usability test might ask users to complete a task using a certain feature in a mobile app. The test might prove that the feature is too hard to use, but it won't say whether users would want to use the app in the first place. (This helps explain why the MyFord Touch design process failed, despite including some task-based research. I'll say more about this in the next chapter.)

Another drawback to usability research is its emphasis on tactical, small-bore details, to the exclusion of larger, more important issues. This can cause practitioners to fail to "see the forest for the trees." For example, a client once described a final report written by a usability consultant her company had hired. She said her team was making their way through the consultant's *200-page* report, which was mainly a list of comments and suggestions about tactical design elements in the product. There was no prioritized list of findings. The usability perspective commonly has this drawback: by focusing on the tiny, detailed problems in an interface, one can miss the larger, more important strategic issues.

Task-based usability can play an important part in strategic work, as long as the usability test is run *after* the strategic context has already been established. Unfortunately, it's common to see companies employing usability improperly, running their users through a battery of prewritten tasks, and missing the larger insights that would be available with a better testing method.

Task-based usability might have been perfect for pilots in the 1950s, but it has limited use today. There's a better way to run research, and it generates a key insight: unmet needs. The next chapter describes what that's all about.

CHAPTER 5 SUMMARY

This chapter examines usability, a research method that focuses on the "actual," in contrast to the previous chapter's look at "hypothetical" methods.

KEY POINTS

- The MyFord Touch story shows the limitation of task-based research: it can only generate insights within predefined limits.
- The B-17 story illustrates the value of taking the user's perspective (as Chapanis did) and having non-directed conversations with users (as Fitts and Jones did).
- Task-based usability can be helpful to deliver tactical improvements, but it cannot set the strategic context.

6

UNMET NEEDS

"Where's the sign?"

Think back to the last time you went to see your doctor. Was it a good experience, designed with your needs in mind? If it was a typical primary care office, you might have checked in with a receptionist seated behind a frosted-glass partition, then sat down in a sterile, unattractive waiting room. Chances are you were kept waiting until well past the scheduled appointment time before finally being seen by a doctor who seemed to be in a rush to finish the visit.

It's easy to list what's wrong with the patient experience in America today, and not just in primary care. Ask just about anyone for a patient story and you'll get an earful about Byzantine processes, mountains of paperwork, doctors who don't take the time to listen, and insurance premiums that go up and up. Patients, doctors, nurses, and administrators all share a sense of frustration and helplessness. And because of the sheer complexity and inertia of the system, it's difficult to imagine any improvement.

But change is possible. In certain primary care offices in San Francisco, New York, and other cities, patients walk into a reception area that looks more like the entrance to a spa or high-end boutique hotel. Friendly, relaxed receptionists sit at an open-air desk, without partitions, and invite patients to sit in a comfortably designed waiting area. Miraculously, the doctor almost always appears on time. What's more, visits can be booked online, and doctors are available to answer questions via email. This is not a high-priced concierge service costing thousands of dollars. Members pay an annual fee of a couple hundred dollars.

The company behind this remarkable network of primary care offices, One Medical, was founded by Dr. Tom Lee in 2005. After earning degrees in both medicine and business, and launching a successful health care software product, Lee was well positioned to change how primary care is delivered. Rather than conforming to the existing structures and incentives of primary care, Lee started One Medical with a radically different perspective.

Early in his career, as an idealistic medical student, Lee had a formative patient experience that helped inspire his plans for One Medical. He explained it this way at Gel, my conference spotlighting people who create good experiences:

> During my first year of medical school, I needed a new pair of glasses. I thought, I'll just schedule an appointment with the ophthalmologist down the hall. I check in and start waiting. Ten minutes go by, twenty minutes, thirty minutes. I'm thinking, I have to go back to class, I've got cadavers to cut. Am I going to be seen?
>
> About forty-five minutes in, I'm finally taken back to the exam room. Great, I thought, finally I can see the doctor. But I sit in the exam room another five, ten minutes. Finally the doctor comes in and they put me through a test, with not a lot of dialogue. More people come in, more tests. I go down the hall, they stick needles in me, start flashing lights in my eyes. It's a crazy experience. The end result was that I never found the results of my tests. I called but never got an answer. To this day I still don't know the results.

Many readers will no doubt be acquainted with these issues: an appointment starting late, a chaotic plan of care, and never learning the outcome of tests. The flagrantly bad experience galvanized the young Tom Lee: "I [had] these ideals of what a patient experience should be like, but I'm thinking, if this is what I'm getting as a med school student, I can't imagine what other people are getting." Years later he would meet this problem head-on by designing One Medical's primary care experience from the perspective of patients.

It's important to note how Lee designed One Medical with patients' needs in mind. In this sense, the innovation process resembled Steve Jobs' work on the iPhone. Lee had to "work backwards to the technology," to use Jobs' phrase. When I asked him how One Medical can afford to provide this patient-friendly care, he explained that the model works because "our administrative overhead is one-third that of most doctors' offices, despite our providing several times the service. This is harder to achieve than people realize—but that's why there's such a big gap between concept and reality in customer experience." At One Medical, technology is designed and deployed specifically to be in service of the patient experience.

There are, of course, countless companies and organizations trying to innovate within the health care system today. Many create technology to comply with new standards or protocols, such as electronic health records. Others focus on one aspect of the patient experience, like billing or plan of care, and offer an incremental improvement over existing solutions. While helpful, these are by definition limited in their ability to improve the overall patient experience. Tom Lee created One Medical to address a much broader scope—the entire primary care experience—with a customer-inclusive approach:

- observing (and directly experiencing!) the delivery of primary care,
- identifying the *key unmet needs* in the patient experience, and finally,
- creating a strategy that focused the organization on delivering on those needs.

Earlier chapters discussed, at some length, the importance of directly observing customers. This chapter focuses on the second step, that of identifying key unmet needs. In particular, I will explore how to go from direct observation to an understanding of those needs. The discussion of research methods can be extended, in fact, to include this thought: *A good research method will reveal customers' key unmet needs.*

This is not to suggest, of course, that innovators should merely ask customers what they want. Instead, good research is based on direct observation of customers, which in turn allows the team to infer the key unmet needs. I'm not the first to point this out. Peter Drucker wrote about the importance of identifying and acting on unmet needs in his 1973 book *Management*, stating that executives must determine "which of the consumer's wants are not adequately satisfied by the products or services offered him today."

Drucker explains his assertion with a case study about Sony, which achieved success early in its history with portable transistor radios. The transistor was an American invention, having been developed by Bell Labs. So why was it a company in Japan, rather than America, that managed to create the breakthrough innovation? Drucker explains:

> The Bell Laboratories people, as well as all the electronic manufacturers in America, had decided that the customer was not yet ready for transistorized equipment. They looked at the wants of the customer that were satisfied by the existing equipment . . . Sony, by asking "What are the unsatisfied wants?" identified a new growth market— and within an incredibly short period established itself worldwide as the leader and the pacesetter.

The key to Sony's insight was direct customer observation. All over America young people were going on picnics and camping trips, and bringing their music with them. This meant lugging an unwieldy, and fragile, piece of equipment down to the beach or camp-site. Customers were willing to put up with this hassle only because there was no alternative. While American manufacturers comfortably reviewed their sales numbers, Sony watched customers in action and saw the massive opportunity of an unmet need.

Sony's little transistor radio had an impact well beyond its heyday. Readers over the age of forty will remember its hugely popular successor, the Sony Walkman, which in turn was the precursor to the iPod. It's fascinating to consider the connections between these devices. Apple's enormously successful products like the iPhone— which was, as we saw, designed with customers' unmet needs in mind—are themselves the descendants of Sony's original radio, which was created using the same mindset. Think about it: some of the biggest successes in consumer technology, from the 1950s through the present day, began with the humble act of finding out what people want.

This idea isn't limited to the technology industry, of course. A focus on unmet needs can bring about transformation in all kinds of places. The following case study shows a perfect example.

THE PROSPECT PARK CASE STUDY

One of the greatest urban turnarounds in recent years was brought about by the simple act of walking through a park. It's a story that deserves to be much better known, if only because it shows the tremendous power of spending time with customers.

Amidst the urban cityscape of Brooklyn lies a vast expanse of trees, grass, hills, and lakes that is Prospect Park. Designed in the 1860s by Frederick Law Olmsted and Calvert Vaux, the park nestles within a meandering diamond-shaped border, offering visitors a surprising range of landscapes and vistas. Olmsted and Vaux's original vision for Prospect Park was to give visitors "a sense of enlarged freedom" to offset the "cramped, confined and controlling circumstances of the street of the town." As an oasis in the middle of a busy, growing metropolis, the park was an immediate success when it opened, attracting millions of residents to enjoy its picturesque beauty—on foot, on horseback, and in carriages (for passengers to see and be seen—the social scene of 1860s Brooklyn!).

After thriving for several decades, the park began a long decline. World War II brought on a sharp decrease in park funding, as well as the construction of barracks and anti-aircraft batteries on park land. In the years following the war, the park suffered through a long period of indifferent or incompetent management. The bottom came during New York's economic crisis in the 1970s. Crime in and around the park had turned Prospect Park into a danger zone, a one-square-mile territory that was best for law-abiding citizens to avoid. In 1979 the park had fewer than two million visitors, the lowest count in many years.

In 1980 the city tried something bold and hired a young new administrator for the park. Tupper Thomas, a thirty-five-year-old urban planner from Minnesota, had responded to a newspaper job post. Despite her lack of experience—and her misspelling of Olmsted's name in her application—Thomas showed an unmistakable spark of energy. (The parks commissioner later said that she "seemed to have come from the moon.") Once hired, she set right to work on what some must have seen as a hopelessly quixotic task: bringing Prospect Park back to life.

It was hard to imagine what would turn things around. After years of neglect, the park badly needed investment—but the city was near bankruptcy. New Yorkers avoided the park because they didn't want to get mugged. These were long-standing, systemic problems without any easy or obvious answer. What could a young, unknown, inexperienced park administrator do?

Other park administrators might have simply asked for more police patrols, or just ignored the problems and passed them along to their successor. (Indeed, that seems to have been the approach in previous years.) Thomas did something different: she went outside. In the first of many brilliant actions during her tenure, she made an effort to spend time with the people who were still using the park.

There weren't many. The most loyal group were the dog owners, locals who wanted to walk with their pets on green grass, away from dull gray concrete. Thomas began observing them as they entered the park, and as she would do throughout her career at the park, she would strike up conversations along the way. She learned their names, their dogs' names, where they lived in the neighborhood, and—most importantly—what they valued. It became clear through these conversations that many dog walkers felt affection for Prospect Park, despite all its flaws. Some even felt a sense of ownership.

But there was a recurring complaint. The law required that dogs stay on the leash at all times. Owners had no legal way to let their dogs run after a ball or tear off across a field. It was frustrating to walk into the park, be surrounded by a vast green space, and still have to keep the dog within arm's reach. This gave Thomas an idea.

Despite the crime in the park, despite the city's economic trouble, and despite her own lack of experience and resources, Thomas sensed an opportunity to actually improve the experience of visiting Prospect Park. Among her remaining "customers," there was one major key unmet need.

She took a gamble. Setting aside the many other concerns and challenges of the park, Thomas focused all her resources on delivering what the dog walkers most wanted—revised leash laws—and it worked. Thomas soon established leash-free zones within the park, and for the first time in years, there was good news in Prospect Park. The visitor count began to rise.

This crucial milestone in Prospect Park's turnaround was made possible by Thomas's approach. Consider how she accomplished all three steps in the "customers included" process, as she –

- got out of the office and observed (and chatted with) park visitors,
- discovered what they wanted most, and then
- focused her resources on making that specific improvement to the visitor experience.

The new leash laws had a cascading impact on the park. The dog owners, seeing that someone was willing to improve things for them—a rarity in New York in those days—helped form a base of support. The dog walkers, in turn, made the park feel safe for joggers, which then attracted the ball players. Soon Thomas would create the Prospect Park Alliance, a group of neighborhood residents and other funders contributing to an endowment for improvement and upkeep.

At last the park was solidly on the way to recovery.

By the mid-2000s, with the help of the Prospect Park Alliance and other groups, Thomas had brought about a full-scale transformation of the park. Visitors entered the park without fear of crime. The grounds were safer, cleaner, and more beautiful. Pathways were repaired, expanses were landscaped. The park now included a restored carousel, rebuilt tennis courts, and an Audubon Center, the first of its kind in an urban setting, situated beside a lake where visitors could rent rowboats from a renovated boathouse. Perhaps most impressively, annual visitors topped nine million in 2009—more than quadrupling the count when Thomas had arrived thirty years before. And more plans for development were being considered.

Meantime, the park's surrounding neighborhoods were undergoing their own transformation. Having been priced out of Manhattan, increasing numbers of young professionals were moving to Brooklyn and bringing with them the coffee shops and boutiques that accompany gentrification. Sights like these represented a tremendous victory not just for Tupper Thomas, but for Brooklyn itself. It's easy to imagine a very different history for the neighborhoods around the park, had a less capable manager taken over in 1980. Brooklyn might not have seen all the energy, optimism, and money that now poured into the borough.

Now Thomas faced the challenge of managing the park's success. Prospect Park needed new development to remain relevant and attractive to its growing visitor population. Diversity was a concern, too: it wouldn't do for the park to become a collection of experiences that were accessible only to wealthy white-collar residents. Multiple priorities were competing for a limited development budget. The park needed a plan.

As Thomas and the board of the Prospect Park Alliance weighed the issues, Creative Good offered to get involved, on a pro-bono basis, to help create a new strategy. Instead of brainstorming ideas while sitting in the board room, charting the way forward would require the steps Thomas took in 1980: getting outside, talking to park visitors, and then focusing resources on what they wanted most. Thomas and the board agreed, and we got right to work.

CREATIVE GOOD GOES TO PROSPECT PARK

Armed with notepads, pens, and a video camera, a team from Creative Good, accompanied by Thomas and other board members, entered Prospect Park on its busiest day of the year: July 4th. Our goal that day was simply to observe how people were using the park.

The weather on this July 4th was as good as one could ask for: sunny and clear, without the stifling humidity that is so common during Brooklyn summers. Barbecues were numerous—Prospect Park allows them, unlike many other New York City parks—and many families were enjoying the holiday while gathered around picnic tables and folding chairs.

The team struck up conversations with several visitors. One resident who appeared to be in his late twenties declared that he had been coming to Prospect Park for years, though only for his family's annual barbecue. We asked if he had ever explored further into the park. (No.) Could he name any other features or spots in the park that people might want to visit? (No.) Then we asked if he'd accompany us on a short walk. (Yes.)

Within a few minutes we showed him the carousel, the boathouse, and the lake. His surprised response made for great video: "I've lived here for, like, sixteen years, and I never knew all the good things they have for kids and adults . . . Snacks, carousel for the kids, the boat house—funny thing is, everything is close, right near each other." He lived within a five-minute walk from the spot where he stood, yet this was his first time seeing the boathouse. "I'll be coming back on Sunday," he concluded.

People just didn't know what was inside the park. We saw this again and again that day, and on subsequent days of research. The Prospect Park Alliance had invested millions of dollars to restore and enrich the park for all Brooklyn residents—yet few of them were aware of what lay outside the small slice of the park that they frequented.

This was partly due to the design of the park. Olmsted and Vaux's original plans created a "rim road," a kind of beltway circling the periphery of the park, suitable for horse carriages. It also served the purpose of separating the outer edges of the park from the interior, which was to be left wild. Thus areas where families now barbecued on July 4th were *meant* to appeal to the majority of visitors, while the interior was intended for the few adventurous souls who wanted to cross the rim road into the forest.

The challenge was that all of the board's recent investments were inside the rim road. The boathouse, the Audubon Center, and the rest were great destinations—for the people who knew about them. Indeed, everyone we brought to those places on July 4th was enthusiastic about what they saw. But they hadn't known about those places until we told them.

And there was another problem. The walking paths winding through the park interior made navigation a challenge. Merely raising awareness about the park's contents might not be enough to solve the problem. We wondered whether visitors could find their way around the park, even if they knew what lay inside.

To answer this question, the Creative Good team returned to Prospect Park for a second round of research. This time we recruited respondents and asked them to meet us at an entrance to the park. When they arrived, we described the Audubon Center—as they might hear about it from a friend—and asked them to find their way there. Then we turned on the video camera and followed along.

The results were just as we had feared: our video footage showed disoriented people scouring various maps and signs, hoping in vain for some hint at the right direction to walk in. In one clip, a bearded man in his sixties peers down at the paper map in his hands. "OK now, here's the Esdale Bridge," he says, indicating a place on the map. "Is that where we are?" He looks down at the wooden bridge he stands on. "Is this labelled, the bridge?" He looks back at the map. "I'm just trying to figure out—where's the sign?" Pretty soon he gives up on finding the Audubon Center.

In another clip, a young couple looks at a map posted at the park entrance. After discussing the map for a few minutes, the woman announces, "We've figured out a route." They walk a few meters into the park and then stop abruptly. In front of them are signs pointing in three different directions. The couple squints at the signs—with tiny, hard-to-read inscriptions—and spots one mentioning the Audubon Center. The sign points straight into dense brush. "Clearly there's no path there," says the man. They eventually give up.

One more clip shows a man in his early thirties somewhere inside the park, standing under a signpost and peering down at a foldout map. He looks up at the signpost, then down at the map. Up at the sign, down at the map. "I'm going to go that way," he says, seeming to choose a random direction. "I didn't see a sign for Audubon."

What's remarkable about these clips is that these people had the sole job of making it to the Audubon Center. No kids in tow, no picnic gear to carry, no distractions that a normal visitor might have. They were totally focused on getting there. And they all failed.

Our two rounds of research clarified that there were two unmet needs for Prospect Park visitors:

1. *Visitors didn't know what was inside the park.* Staying within a familiar area on the periphery, most visitors weren't aware of what was located a few minutes' walk into the interior.
2. *People couldn't find their way.* Even if they tried to get to a particular destination, the confusing or non-existent signage often made navigation impossible.

I will stress here that these insights came from, and in fact *had* to come from, direct observation. It would have been very difficult to fully understand people's experience of Prospect Park had we asked them to answer some survey questions or voice an opinion in a focus group—let alone if we had dreamed up hypothetical scenarios from fictional personas. Even if we had employed a clever brainstorming method, writing ideas on a whiteboard and sketching out possible solutions on Post-It notes, we would have failed without spending time observing park visitors in person.

The key to improving Prospect Park—both times—was the act of including the customer. By walking in the park with people, just as Tupper Thomas had done three decades before, we were able to encounter the full, factual reality of the visitor experience. From there it only required common-sense analysis to see what was preventing people from enjoying the park's benefits.

With this in mind, the Creative Good team presented our proposed strategy to the board. It was focused on one strategic idea, what we call a "hook," which charts a direction for all the supporting recommendations. Stemming directly from the two unmet needs we had discovered—awareness and navigation—our hook was this: *Show visitors what else is in the park.* If the park could expose its offerings to more of its visitors, and show them how to get there, the results would improve both usage and membership numbers—both important metrics to the Prospect Park Alliance.

Some board members were skeptical at the beginning of the Creative Good presentation. (As is usually the case, the skeptics were mainly those board members who hadn't attended the research sessions.) One pointed out that our observations would be normal at any urban park, as visitors everywhere tend to stay near the outer borders. The separation of rim and interior was hardly unique to Prospect Park.

The mood in the room changed when we played a selection of video clips from our research. Board members watched as visitors studied conflicting signs, only to set off in the wrong direction. Other clips showed visitors expressing surprise and delight when they were finally shown the boat house. The video had an immediate and transformative effect. Suddenly the problems with "visitors on the periphery" wasn't some abstract problem that other parks had. It wasn't even just one of many possible issues to weigh against each other within the strategy discussion. By watching the visitors themselves, the board understood that the visitor experience was *the* issue, and it had to change.

And it did change. Within a few months of that presentation, the Prospect Park Alliance launched a new promotional campaign: "Discover the Prospect Park you don't know." This was accompanied by improved park signage, better printed materials, and new online guides to the park. Thus a single project, spanning a little over a month, produced a new focus for the park, and a consensus on the board to implement it. And it all was centered on a few days' worth of direct observation of park visitors.

In the Creative Good project, and especially in Tupper Thomas's groundbreaking work starting in the 1980s, the park was transformed by simply *spending time with people and finding out their unmet needs.* If this seems like an obvious conclusion, think again. There's a good deal of confusion surrounding unmet needs: what they are, how to go about identifying them, and why they're so important in the first place. To clear things up, let's first define the term.

ABOUT "UNMET NEEDS"

At first it may seem difficult to say what, exactly, qualifies as an "unmet need." Is it something customers already know they need, or something they don't know they want until they see it? Is it a desire for a tactical fix, or is it a wish for a systemic improvement? What if someone doesn't literally *need* it but merely wants it—does that even count as a need? Perhaps we should draw out a matrix with all the permutations: known needs, not-yet-known needs, known wants, tactical wanted unknowns, and so on. Thankfully, there's an easier way. Once again I'll point to Peter Drucker's book *Management*, which neatly clarifies the issue with a single concept.

The only purpose of a business, Drucker writes, is "to create a customer"—and that means satisfying some customer need. Perhaps the customer was already aware of the need, "like food in a famine." Perhaps the customer wasn't aware of the need until the solution appeared, like "a Xerox machine or computer." Or perhaps the need didn't even exist until "innovation, credit, advertising, or sales-manship" created it. These are all different types of unmet needs, but Drucker draws no distinctions between them. Instead, he writes, in *all* cases, the single purpose of a business is to fulfill the customer's need.

Drucker's words are a refreshing antidote to the common sugges-tion that customers "don't know what they want" and should be ignored. Drucker says, in effect, it doesn't matter whether customers know what they want or not; either way, it's the company's responsi-bility to discover an unmet need and fulfill it. That is, after all, the only reason the company is in business in the first place.

When I speak to executives and product managers about including customers, I almost always get a question about unmet needs: "Why should we spend time with customers if they don't know what they want?" Or this variation: "How are we supposed to include customers if we want to create something beyond what they can imagine?" These types of questions are especially popular with teams that are determined to produce amazing, world-changing innovations that no one, least of all everyday customers, could possibly have thought of before.

The problem with these questions is their assumption that spending time with customers means asking them what they want. And of course that's a bad idea: as discussed in Chapter 3, Steve Jobs knew that asking customers what they wanted in a smartphone would never have yielded the iPhone. My answer to these questions, therefore, is simple: There's a big difference between *asking* customers what they want and *finding out* what they want. This difference is highlighted in the next story.

A BETTER MEASURING CUP

"Identifying pet peeves is 70% of our challenge," says Alex Lee, president of OXO, a U.S.-based creator of easy-to-use kitchen tools and other housewares. People's unmet needs, or "pet peeves," in the kitchen have formed the basis of a long list of popular OXO products: salad spinners, vegetable peelers, apple corers, and the like. Speaking at my Gel conference, Lee described how direct customer research helped OXO and its design partners at Smart Design Worldwide in the process of creating the OXO measuring cup. The ingenious design—originally conceived by a small toy design firm called Bang Zoom—features lines printed at a sharp angle around the cup, allowing the user to read the measurement from a standing position. This is a distinct advantage over other measuring cups, as OXO and Smart Design discovered during research.

Researchers brought customers, one at a time, into a room outfitted with a sink and an everyday measuring cup, so that they could be observed using the cup. First, though, the researchers asked them a simple question: What's wrong with your measuring cup? Customers had some answers ready: the handle can be slippery, especially if your hands are greasy, and if it's made of glass it can shatter if you drop it. Pouring hot liquids can also make it uncomfortable to hold. Researchers made a point of noting these responses, then asked: Anything else? No, the customers said, that's everything we can think of.

The OXO measuring cup. (OXO)

The researchers then asked each customer to show how he or she used the measuring cup at home. Lee reports that each customer would pour water into the measuring cup, then bend down to check whether the water was at the desired level. Then the customer would pour in a bit more, then bend down again. Pour, bend down, pour, bend down—several times. To the researchers, the pattern was easy to see and it pointed directly to the customers' unmet need. But to the customers, the unmet need was invisible: not one of them indicated that this was a problem. As Lee puts it, "people don't realize that there's a problem until they see the solution."

Because of this direct customer research, OXO and Smart Design were confident that this design solved a key unmet need—even though customers, when asked directly, were unable to describe what the problem was. In other words, OXO didn't just *ask* customers what they wanted. Instead, by observing customers directly, they *found out*.

ABOUT LEAN AND AGILE

In their attempt to find out what customers want, many teams are constrained by the development method they use. "Rapid iterative" methods like Lean and Agile can, by their very structure, limit the impact customers can have on a strategy. These methods are so popular today that they merit some discussion.

Not long ago at a gathering of technologists in New York, I ran into an acquaintance—I'll call him Bob—who is well known among Internet startup entrepreneurs. What would it take, I asked him, to convince a startup company to spend time with users before building its product? Bob answered emphatically that it wasn't necessary: "When they built the Golden Gate Bridge, they didn't start by looking for people swimming across the bay, they just built the bridge." Bob seemed to suggest that innovation would be slowed down by muddling about with customers. The way to succeed, he said, was to be "agile" and start building.

Bob is not alone in his thinking. Of all of the values shared by Internet startups (and, increasingly, larger companies) today, one of the most common is the idea that success comes from moving fast. This worldview is perhaps nowhere better expressed than in Eric Ries's bestselling book *The Lean Startup*, which has inspired startups and teams worldwide to innovate with the Lean approach. (Agile, mentioned in Bob's comment above, is a popular software-development method that closely resembles Lean.)

The Lean model is centered on a cycle of "rapid iteration." This involves launching a new product quickly, measuring customer response, then swiftly incorporating changes to relaunch—that is, "iterate"—the product. In one case study, Ries explains that for teams following the Lean approach, "the focus . . . is iterating with customers as rapidly as possible." This is a concise description of Lean and is best understood in two parts.

On the one hand, Lean means iterating *with customers*. There are no hypotheticals here, no vague opinion-based questions or fictional personas. Instead, when considering a change to the product, the team must first test it out with real-life customers to see if they validate the idea. This is what I like the most about Lean: it actually includes customers.

Then there's the second part of the description, iterating *as rapidly as possible*. The first milestone in the Lean cycle is the launch, as soon as possible, of a "minimally viable" version of the product, after which customer input guides changes to the product before the relaunch. Ries writes that the "speed through [this] feedback loop" is the "core advantage" of Lean teams. Using Lean, a team's interactions with customers take place in a development cycle with a constant emphasis on *speed*.

Naturally, Lean tends to be a good choice when time is short. Consider the example of a team that had just one month to invent, develop, and launch a new iPad game. (The book *Lean UX* by Gothelf and Seiden describes this exact situation.) With the deadline quickly approaching, there was no sense trying to divine customers' "unmet needs" by spending lots of time watching iPad users play games. Instead, using the Lean model, the team quickly generated a game idea on its own and began developing the app almost immediately. Play-testing sessions with customers were used along the way to validate design decisions; anything that didn't test well was changed quickly, thus fulfilling Lean's goal of rapid iteration. The game launched on time.

Lean worked in this case because it forced the team to start development right away, without spending undue time on formal specifications and other traditional steps. But this "build then iterate" approach doesn't work in all circumstances. Specifically, if customers' unmet needs are overlooked when development starts, rapid iteration is unlikely to save the product.

In many projects, by the time development starts, the strategic context is solidly in place. MyFord Touch, from the previous chapter, provides a good example. The design team's "many months" of brainstorming yielded a futuristic touchscreen prototype that set a contextual frame around the customer research that followed. No amount of rapid iteration with customers could reveal the key insight, *outside* that firmly established context, that Ford drivers might prefer to keep their traditional, decidedly non-futuristic dashboard buttons.

During their conference presentation talking about the project, the MyFord Touch designers proudly noted the speed of their process, saying "the design cycle was minutes," and "this way of rapid prototyping and rapid working allowed us to effect change really quickly." Yes, this blazing speed let them do things fast, but the outcome showed the fundamental flaw in that approach. Without fully understanding customers' needs, a Lean team is liable to iterate rapidly toward the wrong solution.

To be clear, I'm not saying that Lean totally ignores customers' unmet needs. Much like task-based usability, covered in the last chapter, Lean *does* uncover unmet needs. It's just that they tend to be the tactical and incremental sort that can be uncovered in a quick interaction. This is the key drawback of the Lean model. Once the team starts rapidly cycling through the Lean iterations, there's not enough time or depth in the process to discover any *strategic* insights about customers' unmet needs. To put it bluntly, you can't iterate your way to a strategy.

In contrast to MyFord Touch, which was a flawed product created through rapid iteration, consider the Toyota Sienna, a very successful minivan created with a different sort of process. Yuji Yokoya, a product manager at Toyota, was tasked in the early 2000s with creating a new minivan that would be more appealing to customers than the other vehicles on the market.

Rather than embarking on a Lean process of rapid iteration, Yokoya did something extraordinary. Before he began designing the minivan, he left his office in Japan and spent weeks driving over 50,000 miles around North America in order to observe typical customers. Along the way, Yokoya discovered the one key strategic insight that would lead the Sienna design: the minivan needed to create a good experience for kids. Parents were buying the minivan for the benefit of their children—keeping them safe, comfortable, and entertained—and so the needs of the child passengers, more than any other factor, would drive the purchase decision. Yokoya took this strategic finding back to Japan and used it to form the basis of the Sienna design.

One reason for the Sienna's huge commercial success, therefore, was the time Yokoya spent with customers before the design process began. Interestingly enough, the Sienna case study appears in Eric Ries's book *The Lean Startup*. Even an advocate for rapid iteration, it seems, can acknowledge that some projects should start with careful observation of customers.

Significant, high-stakes projects tend to fare poorly if strategic insights aren't part of the process. Consider the examples I've already covered: A company makes a major investment in a radically new service (Google Wave). A startup develops a product that will have a significant effect on its users' lives (the Playpump). A government agency embarks on an expensive upgrade to its capabilities (the border fence). In each case, it would have been far better to spend time upfront with customers, before starting development, to generate key insights: who are the customers, what do they need, what do they already have that is working well, what might be the nature of the solution, and so on. I would argue that the failures of Google Wave, the Playpump, and the border fence occurred precisely *because* the teams didn't involve customers in this way. By not discovering their customers' unmet needs, the teams inevitably created something customers didn't want.

The Lean method, then, is an excellent way of quickly getting tactical feedback on an existing idea, whether generated by the team or by some customer-inclusive process. However, Lean is generally not a good choice for projects that need to discover strategic unmet needs. To put it another way, meaty problems aren't always suitable for a Lean solution.

CONCLUSION

We now know what is required in a method that wants to include customers: it must focus on the actual, not the hypothetical; and it must have some capacity to discover customers' unmet needs. What would the method look like? Tupper Thomas's work gives a clue— she just went out and talked to people. And in the previous chapter, Fitts and Jones achieved great success with their open-ended conversations with pilots. I'm now ready to describe the method Creative Good pioneered to help companies include the customer. It's called the listening lab.

CHAPTER 6 SUMMARY

This chapter explains the importance of finding out what customers want—or, as I put it, discovering customers' key unmet needs.

KEY POINTS

- Tom Lee designed his company to address patients' unmet needs in primary care.

- Peter Drucker wrote about unmet needs in 1973, saying that executives should discover customers' "wants [that] are not adequately satisfied by the products and services offered today."

- Tupper Thomas began the amazing turnaround of Prospect Park by talking to the people using the park and discovering their unmet needs.

- There's a big difference between *asking* customers what they want and *finding out* what they want. The story of the OXO measuring cup serves as a good example.

- Lean, and other rapid, iterative methods like it, are helpful for developing prototypes and quickly getting feedback. However, that leaves less time in each interaction with customers, which effectively restricts their input to a tactical level.

7

WHAT CUSTOMERS DO

"When I buy a computer, I want the whole thing."

As a technology reporter for the *New York Times*, Nick Bilton covers the newest mobile apps and digital devices emerging from the technology industry. While he typically writes about these high-tech products from the stance of an industry insider, in the fall of 2011 he wrote a column with a totally different perspective, brought about by an unusual experience he had one day at lunch.

Bilton was at a restaurant with his sister when, in the middle of the meal, she spontaneously decided to use the Twitter app on her phone for the first time. Interested to see how she fared with the app, Bilton "sat inquisitively watching her navigate Twitter. I didn't offer any guidance, although she clearly needed it." His sister promptly flailed around in the app, revealing points of confusion in the Twitter interface that Bilton had never noticed before. "Seeing my sister navigate Twitter, I realized why it was so confusing to so many," he wrote. "It finally makes sense to me."

This was a breakthrough for Bilton. Here he was, a technology expert who had been studying, using, and writing about Twitter for years—yet in the space of a couple of minutes, without the use of any special framework or tool, he was able to gain a new level of understanding about the app. Simply by observing and listening to a user different from himself, Bilton discovered insights that he never could have accessed on his own. And these findings were significant. Because he didn't guide or direct his sister during the experience, Bilton knew that her confusion was a true-to-life representation of what millions of other users must be going through.

Whether he realized it or not, Nick Bilton had stumbled upon something that could totally transform how he understood technology. It was something that—unlike any app, gadget, or website he had ever covered—let him see things from the user's perspective. He had run something very close to what I call a "listening lab."

ABOUT LISTENING LABS

Most people already know, innately, how to run good customer research. It's often called "listening." The problem is that research methods tend to complicate matters, emphasizing process over meaning, rarefied knowledge over common sense, leading practitioners to forget what the endeavor is supposed to be about in the first place. Let me establish, then, once and for all, what research is: *Customer research is the process of understanding, and empathizing with, someone else's experience.*

People who have empathy are perfectly suited to conducting customer research. Their willingness to care about the customer allows them to generate insights in practically any situation. Conversely, for people who lack empathy, or choose not to exercise it, no amount of instruction is bound to do much good. Though they may practice the most complicated methods with expert precision, they'll still be blind to the most important truths about the customer experience.

Everything I write about customer research, from this point on, should be understood in this frame. Far more important than any method I describe, or any procedural suggestion I give, is a genuine care for the customer. That is the essential ingredient of all good research and any customer-inclusive process.

With that in mind, I will describe Creative Good's approach to research, the listening lab, starting with a review of what I have already covered. Previous chapters have made the case for what research should, and should not, do. I have made three main points:

- First, there's a difference between what customers *say* and what they *do*. Research is more effective when it focuses on what customers do. Put a different way, observing the *actual* is more helpful than theorizing about the *hypothetical*.
- Second, research must have the ability to uncover customers' unmet needs. It's not enough to test their performance on a battery of prewritten tasks—because while possibly helpful, that sort of research has limited scope. A task-based usability test, for example, can point out the problems in the details of the interface but won't have much view toward how the customer uses that interface in relation to other tools, items, or other phenomena in their surrounding environment.
- Third, good research does not require a complicated method with esoteric terminology, practiced with scientific rigor. Simply spending time with customers—observing and listening to them—can often allow insights to emerge organically. Academic methodologies can be helpful in more specialized circumstances, but I find it usually works quite well to take a simple common-sense approach with research. (As Yogi Berra once said, you can observe a lot just by watching.)

Early on in Creative Good's history, finding that current research methods weren't effective enough for our customer experience work, we developed our own method—listening labs—which we have since used in nearly all our consulting projects. (We called them "listening labs" to clearly distinguish them from other methods like usability and focus groups. Although the labs involve more than "listening," the name was catchy and we've stuck with it.)

Here are some of the key aspects of the method:

- Listening labs focus on *direct observation of actual customer behavior*. We watch (and, yes, listen to) actual people doing actual things, rather than soliciting opinions about hypothetical products or imagining the preferences and behaviors of fictional characters.

- Labs are one-on-one sessions. Specifically, a typical lab session involves a moderator observing a single person while he or she uses a device, app, site, or other product. We do not bring in a panel of other respondents (unless, of course, the experience in real life would involve multiple people). In this sense the physical setup of a listening lab is superficially similar to a usability test, though the moderation style is different.
- Rather than forcing the customer into a contrived scenario or an artificial list of tasks, listening labs attempt to approximate a real-life customer experience that is relevant to each individual respondent. This way, the behavior we observe is as consistent as possible with what happens outside a research setting.
- Listening labs focus on discovering customers' unmet needs. We try to find out what they are not getting from available products or services that would create an opportunity for innovation; at the same time, we try to understand which existing benefits are especially important to customers and should be retained. (In a car, for example, that might be buttons and knobs that are easy for the driver to reach without taking his eyes off the road.)
- Listening labs are ultimately concerned with creating *measurable results*. Just as empathy is the key ingredient to the research, as described earlier, the key outcome of labs is some tangible, measurable benefit for the company and the customer.

Below is an example to show how the method works.

THE GATEWAY LISTENING LABS

This is one of my favorite stories about listening labs, dating from the late 1990s, just as the ecommerce boom was getting started. Although it took place in a very different technology landscape, it is a classic story whose patterns are remarkably consistent with situations that play out on a daily basis in today's business world.

The story is about Gateway, one of the leading computer companies at the time, which was known in part for its distinctive packaging: their PCs all came in boxes adorned with big black cow spots. Seeing more and more of their business being generated online, Gateway hired Creative Good to improve the user experience of the Gateway website—or rather, one specific part of it.

Before calling Creative Good, Gateway leadership had made a large investment in a "configurator," an online tool allowing website users to customize their desired PC by selecting individual components: RAM, graphics card, processor, and so on. A large consulting firm had charged Gateway hundreds of thousands of dollars to build the configurator, stating that complicated supply-chain management software was necessary to make it work. Initial prototypes revealed an ugly and complicated user interface. Gateway hoped that Creative Good would show how to make the configurator a little less painful to use and thus save some of their enormous investment in the tool.

We started the project by interviewing executive stakeholders at Gateway in order to better understand the company's goals. As is usually the case, the interviews uncovered vital context. The company was just beginning a strategic, company-wide shift toward selling to average, non-techie consumers.

Gateway had started in the mid-1980s as a pioneer in customizing computers for hobbyist buyers. Its customers were early adopters conversant in PC jargon, who—knowing RAM from ROM—would order computers with exactly the components they wanted. The new PC buyers now flooding the market were not early adopters, and they typically found the purchase process difficult and confusing. Gateway hoped that the configurator would make its site more consumer-friendly and thus give it an edge over its chief competitor, Dell.

The listening labs brought together two sets of people. First, there were the prospective customers: these were consumers—not hobby-ists—who were in the market for a new PC within the next few months. We hired a recruiting firm to find a dozen or so of these people and schedule them to appear at a suburban research facility for the labs.

We also invited Gateway executives to attend the research. Since they would have to approve any changes that were suggested by the research, we knew that our interactions with the observing executives would be just as important as what happened with the consumer respondents.

On the morning of the listening labs, several Gateway executives sat in the observation room, safely hidden behind a one-way mirror, while I sat in the testing room with the first respondent. Seeing the PC on the table, the respondent instinctively turned toward it, reaching for the mouse in preparation for whatever task I would give him. Instead, I asked the respondent to turn away from the computer. "Let's just chat for a few moments to start," I said. "Did I understand right that you're intending to buy a new PC in the next few months?" Thus began a conversation where I established rapport and asked the respondent to describe how he planned to shop for a PC.

To move into the next phase of the lab session, I asked the respondent to demonstrate what he had just described. "You know how you said you were looking for a new computer for your home office, one that could run that finance application you told me about? Go ahead and take me through the shopping process as you'd do it at home."

The respondent started, and soon enough he found his way to the Gateway site (which was unsurprising, as users had been recruited who were considering Gateway as a possible brand to buy). But once there, he stopped abruptly. The products were described in language that was written for hobbyists, rather than non-techies like himself. He squinted at the screen. "I see here a '9100XL,' but I'm not sure what that is." After clicking around half-heartedly for a few minutes, he gave up and went to Dell's website.

It quickly became apparent that the first respondent was not an outlier. The second respondent, then the third, then the fourth, all had the same disappointing experience. Simply by observing customers' actions—much like Nick Bilton observed his sister using the Twitter app—I was able to understand, without a doubt, that these problems were occurring outside the labs with the wider customer base.

One particularly animated middle-aged respondent—I've never forgotten him—described his experience succinctly. Like the first respondent, he was unable to parse the high-tech product names and component descriptions. I asked a clarifying question: "Can you describe what you're looking for now?" The man sat back in his chair, looked at me, and said, "When I buy a computer, I want *the whole thing.* I want the box, the monitor, and the printer." These were the "components" that non-hobbyists wanted—not the individual chips that the configurator was asking users to choose.

Meanwhile, in the observation room, the Gateway stakeholders watched closely as customer after customer went online, tried to shop for a PC, and then gave up on the Gateway site. It was clear that I was not directing the respondents. Customers were acting of their own volition, not completing artificial tasks, which made their actions—and confusion—that much more significant. As each successive respondent experienced similar frustrations without any direction or leading questions, two inescapable conclusions began to dawn on the executives: the Gateway website was a disaster, and the configurator was totally irrelevant.

By the end of the labs, the configurator was dead. The labs had proved to Gateway leadership that the website needed an approach entirely different from the configurator. This dramatic change of heart was only possible due to their attendance at the labs.

Based on the lab results, combined with our analysis of Gateway's competitive environment and website metrics, Creative Good developed a simple strategy that generated around $100 million in incremental revenue in the first twelve months after launch. The strategy was to show customers "the whole thing": box, monitor, and printer. Working with Gateway's designers, we then created prototypes expressing this strategy, after which they relaunched the site.

The redesigned Gateway website was strikingly simple, presenting three options for computers people could buy: good, better, best. (Years later, Apple adopted a similar design for its ecommerce site, focusing on the consumer's buying experience rather than the products' technical specs. I don't know that Apple was inspired directly by the Gateway site, but I do know that our work demonstrated a better way of selling computers online.)

Listening labs were the key to the success of this project. Had I run the usability test the client asked for, I would have gotten tactical feedback on how the configurator could make tasks easier to accomplish. But listening labs did something different, and bigger: the research pointed to a strategic shift that, once implemented, would generate a strategic-level outcome. And it changed the minds of the decision makers who otherwise might have resisted such a shift.

Unfortunately, despite the significant revenue increase that the redesign brought, about a year later Gateway management embarked on another website redesign. This was driven by a new strategy—as far as I know, not based on any kind of customer insight—and it turned out to be an expensive mistake. The company folded a few years later.

Still, the listening labs had generated tangible benefits for Gateway, and its customers, that lasted for over a year. And it's worth noting the role the organization played in that. As important as it was to observe the customer, my efforts would have been in vain had the decision makers not attended the research. This leads to a very important point: whatever form research takes, the decision makers must play a part. Any method that hopes to include the customer must also include the organization. (I will cover this idea in some detail in the next several chapters, comprising Part 3 of the book.)

USING LISTENING LABS WITH OTHER METHODS

While listening labs are our core research method at Creative Good, we do frequently use other methods and activities—typically after we have run listening labs and discovered customers' unmet needs—to enhance our consulting work. Below I list how, and when, we have found it helpful to join listening labs with other methods.

Usability tests: Within a well-defined context, usability can be very effective. Most commonly this is after listening labs have helped uncover the unmet needs, we've set the strategy, and we need to double-check some details of the experience. For example, in the Prospect Park case study in the last chapter, we directed visitors to find the Audubon Center and measured their task success. But this was only after we observed them in a non-directed environment and created a strategic framework for the project.

Surveys: Much like usability tests, we use surveys in limited contexts. Used correctly, they can be uniquely valuable. We especially like the Net Promoter survey, originally developed by Fred Reichheld and Bain & Company. Presented to customers just after a customer experience, it asks just two questions: first, how likely would you be to recommend the product or service to a friend? And second, why? We have used this type of survey in much of our consulting work. The first question provides a benchmark for comparison with competitors, while the second question—"why?"—yields valuable qualitative insights. In contrast, we tend to steer away from traditional surveys that ask leading questions (as in the drugstore example) or are simply too long for customers to want to fill out.

Personas: As described in Chapter 4, Creative Good does occasionally create a modified version of personas, at a client's request, *after* we run listening labs. In this case, we don't spend any time inventing fictional details, since at that stage we already have real data from real people (and we can use their real names and real photos). Thus personas can serve the useful purpose of summarizing the results of listening lab research.

Rapid prototyping: This can be a fun and engaging way to have the team brainstorm solutions to the problems revealed by research. There are many rapid prototyping activities and exercises to choose from. But I would consider running such an exercise only *after* conducting research to discover customers' unmet needs. What's more, research often reveals such obvious findings that the client doesn't need a brainstorming session to decide what it should do next.

Business analysis: While not a research method per se, an analysis of the business context is so vitally important in Creative Good's project work that I would be remiss in not mentioning it. In order to create tangible value in any project, we need to first understand which outcomes the client considers valuable. And that means we must understand the full context that the project fits into. We typically begin a project with an RFI (request for information) in which we ask the client for all the metrics, strategy documents, past research reports, and any other data or documents that can help set the stage for the customer research that follows. We also typically interview the decision makers and stakeholders in the project, as knowledge on the team can differ from what is recorded in official documents. Finally, wherever possible, we combine all of this knowledge with an in-depth competitive review, to understand where the product or service fits into a more strategic landscape of the industry. None of these steps are particularly novel or innovative. But by combining this knowledge with actual customer research, we're able to generate insights that are both accurate (based as they are on actual customer data) and meaningful (since they emerge in a business context).

Analytics: Creative Good projects often include quite a bit of data analysis, as it's an essential complement to the qualitative work. In the RFI mentioned above, we ask for any relevant analytics data—traffic data for websites or mobile apps, "conversion funnel" data (measuring customers' progress through the stages toward a sale), reports from the team's metrics platform, and so on. Analytics most often come into play at the beginning of a project, helping to set the context of what is actually happening in the business; and then after labs, when analytics often back up the findings from listening labs with statistically significant data. Of course, the data is only as good as the analysis applied to it.

HOW TO JUDGE A METHOD

Before I conclude Part 2, describing "the method," I need to deliver two more insights—a kind of dual punchline to the four chapters in this section. First, while I have advocated for Creative Good's preferred method of listening labs, there are of course many methods available today. Facing this panoply of options, a team may reasonably want a way to evaluate the effectiveness of various methods.

There is only one way to truly judge the effectiveness of any method, and that is by measuring its results. When I ran listening labs for Gateway, for example, the value of the project was measured by the profit the company earned because of the new strategy—not the task success of the website users, and not the academic rigor with which I conducted each research session. The dollars are what mattered to the client. I bring this up because customer research, as it is commonly practiced today, has a tendency to be evaluated by how faithfully it adheres to a kind of platonic ideal of methodology. Some practitioners tend to get wrapped up in the methods themselves, to the exclusion of what the methods are trying to accomplish. I want to set the record straight: *A method is only as good as its measurable results.* If listening labs create the most gain in revenue, or adoption, or savings, then use listening labs. But if even better results come from using task-based usability, or Lean, or any other process, why would anyone hesitate to change to a more effective method? *Results are more important than method.*

Second, I'd like to admit—yes, at the end of "the method" section— that I have failed to completely describe the method. Left mostly untouched is an essential and major component of the customer-inclusive innovation process. Think back: it's important to observe customers directly and discover their unmet needs. But this, by itself, doesn't create the results. (Remember to judge by results, not method!) Generating results means some change has to occur. And the only way any team, company, or organization can change is if the organization itself allows the change to happen. To include the customer, one must also include the organization. Part 3 explores what that means.

CHAPTER 7 SUMMARY

This chapter describes the listening labs method with the case study of Creative Good's project with Gateway, a PC manufacturer.

KEY POINTS

- Customer research is the process of understanding, and empathizing with, someone else's experience.
- The finer points of research methods are less important than whether the researcher has empathy for the customer.
- Having said that, I have found listening labs to be effective. These are non-directed, strategic, open-ended interactions with customers.
- The Gateway case study shows how listening labs allow unexpected findings to emerge. In Gateway's case, customers made it clear that they wanted a very different kind of experience from what Gateway had built.
- Listening labs work well in concert with other methods, which can help set the business context before the labs, and validate or confirm the findings after the labs.

PART 3

THE ORGANIZATION

"We want to include you in this decision without letting you affect it."

8

THE COST OF IGNORING THE ORGANIZATION

"Hoping I don't get fired."

One day in the spring of 2009, a web designer named Dustin Curtis visited the American Airlines website and booked a flight. He didn't like what he experienced, to put it lightly. Curtis was so incensed that he wrote a blog post saying American's website was "terrible," "abusive," and was "permanently destroying the brand and image" of the airline. Curtis is widely read among web designers, and his rant went viral, prompting a host of other bloggers and commenters to join in deploring the sorry state of affairs on AA.com.

Although Curtis didn't state exactly what he hated about the site, he did post screenshots showing a homepage cluttered with a mishmash of links, text, and promotional images. (He also posted his proposal for a simpler, easier-to-use design, which he said took him a couple of hours to create.) While it may not have been "permanently destroying" the American brand, the AA.com homepage was undoubtedly in need of improvement.

Curtis then asked why a well-known company would allow such a design to represent it online: "How does your CEO . . . justify treating customers this way? Why does your board of directors approve of this?" His outrage was palpable. If it required only one designer and a couple of hours to create a superior design, why would American Airlines, with its vast resources, continue to offer such a bad experience? Curtis seemed to suggest that the culprit was incompetence, starting with the CEO, and reaching all the way to the in-house design team—which he said should be fired.

The AA.com homepage in 2009. (Internet Archive)

My main reaction after reading Curtis's post was empathy. I remembered all too well, in the early years of Creative Good, being vexed by the same question. At the dawn of the dotcom era, I wrote "In Search of E-commerce," a report critiquing the websites of Apple, Amazon, Barnes & Noble, and the very first homepage of Expedia. The report described the frustrating experience of shopping and ordering products at these sites and suggested how the companies could fix the glaring errors and immediately increase their online sales. It seemed so simple at the time: companies would read the report, correct the mistakes on their websites, and everyone would benefit.

A different reality emerged soon after the report was released. Although it sold briskly, including to several of the featured companies, the report didn't bring about much noticeable change. Many of the problems it documented were still visible months later. This raised the same question Dustin Curtis would later ask: why would a company frustrate its customers with a bad experience, when an improvement would be so easy to make?

The reality is that a customer experience will improve only if the organization wants to change. Merely pointing out problems won't work. Going a step further and proposing a solution is still no guarantee that the problems will get fixed. Any attempt to create or improve a customer experience requires the support of the organization.

Everything in the book so far has led up to this point. Part 1 explained the importance of directly observing customers. Part 2 described how to discover their unmet needs. In this third and final part, I reveal one more essential step. *To include the customer, you must also include the organization.* This is a vital point that rarely gets discussed.

Despite its fundamental importance, the role that the organization plays in the customer experience has never received much attention from the user experience field. This may have something to do with the field's origins in military and academic research which, as described in Chapter 5, historically focused on the tool rather than any wider context. Consequently, year after year I see user experience conferences, books, blog posts, and papers excitedly describing all manner of research and design methodologies, while saying little or nothing about involving the rest of the organization in the process.

The result is a chronic problem faced by many user experience researchers, interaction designers, and other practitioners. They sense, correctly, that they are limited in the impact they can have. While able to score tactical victories, like improving the usability of a page, screen, or task, they don't have much influence in the organization, or on the product, beyond that scope. Meanwhile, the significant and strategic decisions—what kind of product will be made, for which customers, to accomplish which goals—are almost always made by executives outside the user experience team. And those executives, in turn, have to balance a host of other concerns—political, financial, and operational—when making their decisions. This combination of factors helps explain why companies that employ user experience teams can still create a bad user experience. And that brings me back to the story of American Airlines.

After his post was widely shared online, Dustin Curtis received an email from an American Airlines employee, "Mr. X," who said he worked on the user experience team for AA.com. The reason for the cluttered site design, Mr. X wrote, wasn't the incompetence of anyone at American, as Curtis had suggested. Instead, the culprits were the "culture and processes" within the company:

> The group running AA.com consists of at least 200 people spread out amongst many different groups, including, for example, QA, product planning, business analysis, code development, site operations, project planning, and user experience. We have a lot of people touching the site, and a lot more with their own vested interests in how the site presents its content and functionality . . .

> For example, our Interactive Marketing group designs and implements fare sales and specials . . . the Publishing group pushes content . . . and don't forget the AAdvantage team (which for some reason, runs its own little corner of the site) or the international sites . . . AA.com is a huge corporate undertaking with a lot of tentacles that reach into a lot of interests.

Mr. X concluded by gently chiding Curtis for his naiveté. The problems on the site weren't due to a lack of design skill on the team. Whipping up a new homepage design, he wrote, would be a "piece of cake." Instead, the real challenge facing AA.com was "the momentum even a simple redesign must overcome"—that is, the organization. Mr. X had set Dustin Curtis straight with an accurate assessment of how customer experiences get built in the real world. He concluded by signing his note, "hoping I don't get fired."

Unfortunately, that is exactly what happened. An hour after Curtis posted the response from Mr. X on his blog, American Airlines management identified the employee and promptly fired him. A company spokesman stated that Mr. X had broken his employment agreement by divulging details of the site strategy. (His email to Curtis had been explicit about upcoming feature launches.) Predictably, this brought about another outraged comment from Curtis about clueless leadership at American Airlines.

The episode illuminates some of the obstacles to change in many large organizations. The sheer amount of business complexity means that any change to the customer experience, even a simple one, must often be integrated across multiple systems. Requirements of quality control, business logic, and regulatory compliance (to name a few) can slow the process. And then there is the issue of the people themselves. As the next case study shows, another common barrier to improving the customer experience is a lack of political buy-in.

THE STORY OF ACMECARE

If stakeholders aren't fully on board, even the most well-intentioned effort to benefit customers can encounter serious problems. I saw this several years ago when Creative Good was hired by a large health care organization, which I'll refer to as "AcmeCare," to chart a better customer experience. After conducting several rounds of listening labs with executives present, and a good bit of research into AcmeCare's internal metrics and processes, we synthesized it all to create a simple, compelling, actionable strategy for AcmeCare to move forward. We showed how implementing the strategy would save the company a massive amount of money while creating a much better experience for patients. (The listening labs had revealed that patients wanted a much simpler, lower-cost solution than the expensive, complicated system that AcmeCare was preparing to develop.)

The AcmeCare executives who had hired Creative Good were strongly in favor of the proposed strategy—after all, it would generate significant savings and happier patients. But before they could start implementation, they needed to share the findings with the rest of the organization. They asked us to create a video that described our customer research, the strategy that had come out of it, and the benefits it would bring AcmeCare and its patients. In short order we delivered a polished, well-edited video describing the project and its next steps.

Our stakeholders liked what they saw and immediately began distributing the video throughout AcmeCare. Unfortunately, that didn't last long. A few days after beginning to send around the video, they received an abrupt message from an executive in the communications division: "Immediately halt distribution of the video." Confused, they contacted the executive to ask what the problem was. This was an important project, and AcmeCare and its patients stood to benefit greatly from the new strategy.

The executive told them sternly that the video was unacceptable and couldn't possibly be shared with the wider organization. By proposing changes to the company's service offering, he explained, the video clearly implied that there was something wrong with the organization's current direction. There was no tolerance for such "negative" communications, and it had to be shut down.

The AcmeCare project showed the importance of identifying, and involving, all stakeholders who are affected by a project. Any change, no matter how beneficial, can be seen as a threat to an executive who isn't included in the process.

One outcome of this project was a new policy for Creative Good's consulting work: starting in the sales process, before the contract is signed, I ask prospective clients to agree to invite all relevant stakeholders to the listening labs. If the research doesn't allow full attendance, as in "field research" where only a couple of people can fit into the user's home office, I ask the client to commit stakeholders to watching the videos afterward. Involving the organization from the very beginning of a project allows it to make better decisions later on.

HOW TO INFLUENCE A DECISION

Any significant change to the customer experience requires the organization to make some big decisions, so it's helpful to understand how the process works. Jeffrey Pfeffer, a professor of organizational behavior at Stanford, writes in his book *Power* that organizations have two ways to make decisions, or as he puts it, "resolve the inevitable disagreements about what to do and how to do it":

[either] through the imposition of hierarchical authority in which the boss gets to make the decision, or through a more political system in which various interests vie for power, with those with the most power affecting the final choices.

To get anything done, in other words, you need some support within the organization, from either the boss or an internal faction. Using examples from Machiavelli to Condoleeza Rice, Pfeffer describes how to effectively wield political power in order to gain that support. Much of the book's suggestions are aimed at helping individual executives expand their power base, observing that "likability is overrated" and explaining how to "network with the right people." It's a realistic look at the pragmatic, if somewhat calculated, ways that executives can steer a decision to benefit themselves.

Trying to benefit the customer, however, requires a different approach. There is typically no single executive (except perhaps the CEO) who is the natural advocate for the customer. Instead, the customer experience is usually delivered through the combined efforts of multiple divisions, channels, or service lines. (The tree swing cartoon at the beginning of the book expresses this very idea.) Navigating this medley of groups can make it difficult to effect change, though not because the organization is intentionally opposed to customers. Instead, the internal political structure is organized around silos that are naturally concerned with their own functions, rather than the overall customer experience. Any executive who intends to advocate for the customer, therefore, can't do it alone. The effort requires buy-in from the wider organization.

Pfeffer provides a fascinating case study on this point. Dr. Laura Esserman, a breast cancer specialist at UCSF, began an effort in the 1990s to improve the patient experience with a new facility. She wanted, among other things, to "get the relevant specialties together in one attractive, patient-friendly setting so women did not have to go from place to place, in some instances carrying their own medical tests and records." The internal structure of the cancer center, with surgery and radiology in different departments, didn't lend itself to a patient-centered approach. It wasn't clear where Esserman would find the leverage to change the organization. "Many people," writes Pfeffer, "thought her efforts were doomed."

Yet Esserman succeeded. By 2003 the new facility was open, and by 2009 she had launched a number of other initiatives to improve patient outcomes. Pfeffer writes that it took Esserman years of "dogged persistence" to build the relationships and influence necessary to make her vision a reality. Especially important was her change in attitude as she met opposition. At first she was "quick to anger, impatient, and often neither able nor particularly interested in seeing things from the perspective of others, particularly those she saw thwarting her efforts." But gradually she changed her approach to be more inclusive of the other stakeholders. By seeking common ground and cultivating political allies, little by little, she persuaded the organization to address patients' needs in its delivery of care.

WHY ORGANIZATIONS DON'T DELIVER WHAT CUSTOMERS WANT

Changing any organization for the benefit of the customer is difficult and often lonely work. By their very structure, most organizations are not prone to create customer-inclusive products and services. (The American Airlines and UCSF examples attest to that.) Moreover, executives are vulnerable to any number of influences that can distract them from including the customer in their decision-making. Consider the case studies I've covered so far:

- the organization pursues a "disruptive" strategy (Netflix), while customers want the company to execute on the fundamentals;
- the organization is obsessed with a rival (as Walmart pursued Target), while customers want it to stay true to its core customer experience;
- the organization complacently ignores the changes in its competitive landscape (Bell Labs), while customer behavior clearly reveals unmet needs;
- the organization has been convinced by a vendor to buy an expensive solution (SBInet, Gateway's configurator, the

AcmeCare system), while customers actually want a far less expensive solution to a completely different problem;

- the organization wants to create an "innovative" product (Playpump, Google Wave) or a futuristic design (MyFord Touch), while customers want something useful, simple, functional, and decidedly unsexy.

In each case, the result is that the organization creates what customers don't want. It's not because the organization is actively opposed to customers, but because *organizations never include customers by default*. Delivering a better, more customer-inclusive experience always requires an intentional effort.

This raises an obvious question of process. How, exactly, is an organization supposed to go through this transformation? Laura Esserman demonstrates one very effective way, but most teams don't have several years to spend on the project. They need to take some step now and see a result right away. In order for "customers included" to make any sense at all, there must be some way forward. There must be some catalyst, some lever, to get the organization to start including the customer immediately.

Fortunately, there exists an elegant, surprisingly effective solution. As shown in the next chapter, one simple step can practically work miracles.

CHAPTER 8 SUMMARY

Including customers is not merely the process of observing customers and discovering their unmet needs (as described in Parts 1 and 2). One further step is required: getting the organization on board.

KEY POINTS

- It's not enough to point out the flaws of a customer experience. As Dustin Curtis showed with AA.com, that approach is unlikely to result in any tangible change.

- Any attempt to create or improve the customer experience requires cultivating the support of the organization. In other words, *to include the customer, you must also include the organization.*

- It's important to involve all decision makers who could be affected by a change to the customer experience. Without their support, the effort could fail.

- Organizations never include the customer by default; it requires intentional effort to get the organization to make a customer-inclusive change.

9

CONVINCING THE TEAM

"Go away."

As noted in the last chapter, organizations have a natural resistance to creating a good experience for customers. Before describing the solution we've developed at Creative Good to move clients past that resistance, I want to better define the problem. In particular, let's directly confront the question I posed in the first sentence of the book: Why do companies so often fail to give customers what they want?

The case studies discussed so far have repeatedly made the point that companies tend to fail when they don't include the customer in their decision making. These stories point to a rather obvious conclusion: *Don't totally ignore your customer*. I frequently use this line when speaking to companies, and it usually gets a laugh. After all, who would ever think that ignoring customers would be a good idea?

And yet, as we've seen, many companies still fail to include the customer. So we're still left with this nagging question: why? *Why* are companies naturally resistant to including customers? *Why* is it that, as stated in the last chapter, customers are never included by default?

The best explanation I've found comes from Elting Morison in his classic essay "Gunfire at Sea." Originally delivered as a lecture in

1950, it tells one of my favorite stories of teams resisting change—and describes why it happens.

A LESSON FROM GUNFIRE AT SEA

In 1900, a young American naval officer named William Sims spent some time on a Royal Navy warship, where he was astonished to encounter several improvements the British captain had made to the ship's guns. In those days, gunnery—specifically, how fast and how accurately a ship could fire its guns—was a chief measure of success for all warships. What Sims saw on the British ship were advances in gunnery that he believed could transform the entire U.S. Navy.

HMS Terrible, one of the British ships that pioneered continuous-aim firing.
Photo taken between 1897 and 1899. (Wikipedia)

What were these dramatic improvements? The British captain had solved the primary challenge of gunnery at the time: how to accommodate the roll of the ship—that is, how to properly aim the gun as the ship was pushed about by waves. Naval guns at the time were more or less set in place, thus requiring the gunner to time the shot perfectly, lighting the fuse so that the shell launched at the exact moment the ship was in the right position between the trough and the peak of the wave. This sense of timing took years for gunners to develop, and even then gunnery wasn't very accurate. It also wasn't very fast, since the rate of fire was limited by the periodic cycle of the waves.

The British captain's advance, which Sims wanted to bring immediately to the U.S. Navy, was to allow gunners to counteract the roll through the use of a small hand crank. When the waves pushed the ship up, the gunner could crank the gun down; when the ship rolled down, the gunner could crank the gun back up. By doing so, the gunner could keep the gun aimed constantly at the target. Independent of the waves, the gunner could shoot his gun much more quickly and accurately, achieving what's called "continuous-aim firing." (The captain also improved the telescope-like gun sight attached to each gun, further improving the accuracy of the shots. Previously, the telescope sight had been firmly attached to the barrel of the gun. Any gunner who happened to be looking through the sight when the gun fired would get smacked in the face.)

With the help of the British captain, Sims took these improvements back to his own ship and trained the gunners in continuous-aim firing. The results were immediate and dramatic: within a few months, Sims' ship was reporting much higher accuracy and rate of fire. Having proven that the innovation could be replicated, Sims began his attempt to bring continuous-aim firing to the entire U.S. Navy.

Before we get to what happened next, consider what had happened so far: Sims had proven that he could vastly improve one of the key metrics of the entire U.S. Navy. The innovation was inexpensive to implement and could show results within a short time. There were no obstacles to sharing the innovation widely, like patents or license fees. (In today's language we might say that continuous-aim firing was open-source and easily scalable.) What's more, Sims had amassed tangible, quantitative proof of effectiveness; in fact, he wrote over a dozen official reports documenting what he had accomplished. At first glance, it may seem like it would have been easy for Sims to convince the navy to change. But it wasn't.

After Sims sent off his reports through official channels, he heard back . . . nothing. No response. Morison writes that "the reports were simply filed away and forgotten. Some indeed, it was later discovered, were half-eaten-away by cockroaches."

Instead of giving up, Sims sent a new round of letters, this time using a harsher tone and challenging his superiors to respond. He also sent copies of his reports to other officers throughout the navy, helping to raise awareness of his innovation among his peers. Sims' dogged persistence finally elicited a response from Washington. The answer essentially amounted to this simple statement: "Go away." Sims' superiors assured him that there was nothing wrong with gunnery in the U.S. Navy, that American equipment was just as good as British equipment, and perhaps most pertinently, that Sims couldn't possibly have generated the results he claimed, because continuous-aim firing was impossible.

Sims still refused to stop. Having exhausted all other lines of communication, he wrote directly to President Theodore Roosevelt, who was sufficiently convinced by Sims' proposal that he appointed Sims as the navy's new Inspector of Target Practice. From that point on, Sims gradually but completely transformed naval gunnery to adopt continuous-aim firing.

While it's satisfying to learn that Sims eventually succeeded in his quest, what's more instructive is the response Sims initially received from Washington. Here was an innovation that would vastly improve a crucial capability of the service—and his superiors tried to shut it down. Morison writes:

> Why this refusal to accept so carefully documented a case, a case proved incontestably by records and experience? Why should virtually all the rulers of a society so resolutely seek to reject a change that so markedly improved its chances for survival?

Morison points out that it wasn't due to naval leaders having "blunter minds and less resilient imaginations." Instead, the naval leaders felt threatened by Sims' innovation. Apart from honestly having trouble believing Sims' claims, Morison argues, the officers objected to any interference with their well-ordered world.

Sims' innovation, though it promised to improve gunnery, would also bring about changes that would be painful to accommodate. Crew would have to be retrained on the new equipment, long-standing onboard procedures would have to be modified, and most pertinently, the existing social order might shift to favor younger officers who were enthusiastic about the new development. Facing a prospect of changing their "daily routines, habits of mind, social organization, physical accommodations, conventions, and rituals," Morison writes, the officers exhibited the "normal human instinct to protect oneself, and more especially, one's way of life." This instinct for self-preservation led them to reject an innovation that would have considerably improved their organization's performance.

Something very similar occurred during our AcmeCare project described in the previous chapter. Executives, when faced with our recommendations for improvement, reacted by shutting down the process. Our findings were seen as a threat to the established order, especially since they implied that the executives didn't know every-thing and might need to learn something from people outside the organization (that is, patients). Although the recommendations weren't offered as criticism, they were perceived as such by leaders clinging tightly to the status quo.

Sims himself was seen as a threat. Naval leaders in Washington trivialized his recommendations in part because he was a junior officer, stationed overseas, with no real political capital. Their response of "our equipment is as good as the British," to use Morison's para-phrase, revealed their defensiveness. Feeling vulnerable, the naval leaders reacted strongly against the new approach—much as AcmeCare executives did a century later.

Morison's case study has lost none of its relevance over the years. The business world today may be permeated with digital technology, startups, and talk of disruption, but organizations are still just as resis-tant to change as they ever were. Of course, this is more pronounced in large organizations, like AcmeCare or indeed the U.S. Navy, but even smaller teams are subject to this phenomenon. Many executives, when shown a radically better way of doing things, prefer to continue with business as usual.

The challenges described by Morison should be familiar to anyone who has tried to include customers in an organization not accustomed to doing so. This raises an obvious question. If the prospect of change—even for an improvement that would greatly benefit the organization—naturally generates such resistance, what hope is there to persuade executives to include customers? In other words, how should we go about convincing the team?

At Creative Good we've found one step to be consistently effective. It's described in the next story.

OBSERVING THE ANNOYED CUSTOMER

"I love the company. I tell everyone about them." Sitting with one of our consultants in the research room, the middle-aged man raved about his loyalty to a certain financial services company. Unbeknownst to him, that company was our client, and several of its top executives sat a few feet away, on the other side of the mirrored glass. "I love their website. I look at everything they do," he continued.

Our consultant observed the respondent as he began to use the company's product then in development, an innovative new way to conduct financial transactions online. The client had made a strategic bet on this product and had built out a prototype, then hired Creative Good to evaluate and improve the customer experience.

A few minutes into the interaction, after struggling through the signup process, the respondent's tone changed abruptly. "I'm wondering what the heck they want," he said. "It's kinda ticking me off right now." The man who had previously stated his love for the company went on to say that he would never use the product.

The same transformation was visible in a subsequent respondent, who started off by enthusiastically stating how much she admired the company. A few minutes later, unprompted, she said: "OK, that was confusing. Now I'm very frustrated." The next respondent also had trouble: "I'm a little confused as far as, did I apply, is there an actual, or did I—I'm a little thrown off."

Yet another respondent offered this conclusion: "I guess 'annoyed' is the word that best suits me now." By then, the executives in the observation room might have said the same thing.

This went on for two days: customers who were initially enthusiastic (we had recruited people who felt positively about the brand) abruptly changed their tone when they used the new product. Within a few minutes of trying it out, nearly all of the respondents showed that they were frustrated and ready to quit.

Surprising as it may sound, our client was happy with the research. Despite the disappointment of seeing customers have such negative reactions, the executive who hired us said that this round of research was more valuable than their preceding several months of work on the product. This was due to multiple factors.

First, there was the value of the findings. As described in Chapter 7, listening labs allow customers to demonstrate an authentic, real-life experience with the product, showing what would happen outside the lab setting. Rather than restricting users to the artificial tasks of a tactical usability test, or the opinion-based questions of a focus group, the labs showed what customers actually *did* with the product. (More than one customer had gotten so confused that they made a phone call to product support in the middle of the lab session.) This revealed strategic improvements the team could act on.

Equally valuable to our client was the experience of watching customers in person. Rather than delivering a report about the research after the fact, Creative Good brought executives to the listening labs, allowing them to see for themselves the effects that their decisions were having on customers. It is much harder to ignore customer feedback—or tell someone to "go away," as naval leaders did to Sims—when the truth is plainly visible a few feet away.

Finally, there was the consensus that the labs built among the executives on the team. Like so many organizations, our client was having trouble agreeing on the direction for its new product. Group A, led by executive A, believed in one strategy, with its own priorities and features. Group B had its own executive champion with very different beliefs about what the product should be. The political conflict was playing out in the product design, resulting in a fractured and confusing customer experience.

The listening labs enabled executives on both sides of the conflict to attend, observe, and discuss the same research sessions. Together they watched customers enter the room smiling, flail around with the product, and leave disappointed. After each lab session, our consultant would return to the observation room and ask the executives, "OK, what did everyone see?" As people around the room offered their observations, heads began to nod—on both sides. Discussions back at the office might be politicized, but here at the labs both factions could agree that the customer, a neutral party, was in need of help. For the first time in the history of the product, everyone on the team was agreeing on something. From this foundation we were able to facilitate the team's progression toward a new consensus about the product strategy.

Last chapter I promised "a simple step that can practically work miracles," and here it is: *If you want to convince an organization to include customers, involve the decision makers in the research.* Bringing customers' concerns to the fore can remind everyone that they're already aligned in trying to serve the customer, thus breaking down barriers that prevent decision makers from working together.

CHANGING MINDS THROUGH RESEARCH

At first, it might seem unlikely that customer research could change executives' minds. After all, customers aren't always fun to watch, since their behavior tends to show that they care a whole lot less about a company's product than the executives do. To customers, most products and services are minor items they might use in the course of a day to accomplish some task, find some information, or have some experience—the simpler and easier, the better. As Peter Drucker puts it:

> To the customer, no product or service, and certainly no company, is of much importance. The executives of a company always tend to believe that the customer spends hours discussing their products . . . The customer only wants to know what the product or service will do for him

tomorrow. All he is interested in are his own values, his own wants, his own reality.

There's also the question about the reliability of the research. When describing listening labs to potential clients, I often get asked whether the insights—which are, after all, what the team will build consensus on—can be trusted to be solid and accurate. In particular, they ask, how can a small sample size of a few customers be considered a legitimate source of data? I think it's a fair question, since we're not working with a statistically relevant sample: Creative Good usually runs one day of research for each major customer segment, and as each lab takes about an hour, a typical day includes eight to ten one-on-one sessions. While it might not seem that a handful of customers could generate convincing and actionable insights, I have yet to be asked that question by a client who has already gone through listening labs. This is because, almost without fail, the majority of respondents, without any direction from the moderator, voluntarily reveal strikingly similar insights.

In the Gateway research, for example, customer after customer demonstrated their desire to purchase a "box, monitor, and printer" rather than a configuration of a motherboard and RAM chips. Patterns like this emerge in every context: we've seen it in our research on a media company's mobile app, on a major social network, even on the touchscreen kiosks of a major retailer. It's highly convincing for stakeholders when customers repeatedly have experiences revealing the same problems and the same unmet needs. Consider it from a statistical point of view: in a non-directed environment, an individual respondent has thousands, perhaps millions, of possible responses to a given customer experience. When eight people in a row point out exactly the same issues, there are no skeptics behind the glass. Even then, though, the team still has to build consensus.

BUILDING CONSENSUS

Consensus is never easy to create. Getting a group to agree on anything is difficult, especially when it's a significant decision. (Recall Pfeffer, in the previous chapter, saying that most decisions are made either by the boss or "political interests vying for power.") Consider two common ways, outside the lab setting, in which consensus is created imperfectly or not at all.

First, in the all-too-common situation of political conflict—with, say, Group A seeking one solution and Group B seeking another—each faction may assemble its own data in a process isolated from the other side. Group A gets its consultant to report back its desired message, while Group B may run some directed research to generate the appropriate response from customers (see the car company focus group in Chapter 4). Listening labs eliminate this political maneuvering by bringing all stakeholders together to watch the *same* research. The non-directed nature of the interactions reassures both sides that the customer has not been prepped or manipulated into behaving in a certain way.

The second common situation is when a majority opinion is challenged by a minority, either a small group or a lone dissenter. The healthiest organizations have some structured or acceptable way for dissent to be expressed. Peter Drucker writes that bringing "dissent . . . into the open is in itself salutary," as it addresses "hidden or half-understood disagreements [that] underlie many of the personality problems, communication problems, and irritations that tend to divide a top-management group." But in many teams, dissent isn't so welcome. There is a large body of research on group dynamics, dating back almost a century, documenting how dissent can be suppressed.

One such effect is "groupthink," the tendency of a group to arrive quickly at a decision or consensus while ignoring relevant data along the way. This often means censoring input differing from the majority view. Non-conformers are often vilified or ostracized, as shown by the many whistleblowers who have been rewarded with disapproval or punishment.

Suppressing dissent can have widespread effects. Behavioral scientist Cass Sunstein writes in a 2004 paper about the "failure of deliberation"—that is, the faulty decision-making that groups are prone to—that contributed to the Columbia space shuttle disaster that occurred the year before. The official accident report concluded that "NASA does not appear to embrace . . . alternative perspectives [or] critical perspectives," and as a result, "it is difficult for minority and dissenting opinions to percolate up through the agency's hierarchy." This organizational culture helped create the unsafe conditions that led to the disaster.

Though not as dramatic, there are more common occurrences of this problem. Consider how uncomfortable it is to report a bit of bad news to the boss or the wider team. In situations like these, many people find it easier to shut down, which can cause the group to malfunction. Sunstein writes of "social pressures" that

> lead people to silence themselves in order not to face . . . the disapproval of relevant others. As a result of these problems, groups often do not correct but instead amplify individual errors; . . . fall victim to cascade effects; and tend to end up in a more extreme position in line with the predeliberation tendencies of their members.

Real consensus is impossible for groups that silence or punish the person voicing an unwanted truth. But in listening labs, the dissenting voice can't be shut down, because it's on the other side of a sound-proof glass. The bearer of bad news at listening labs isn't anyone on the team, it's *the customer*. And that makes all the difference.

I think of customers as the trump card at listening labs, because the customer is the one dissenting voice that nearly all executives will agree to listen to. As long as the customer is seen to be non-directed, free from any politically biased coaching, and not constrained by prewritten tasks or questions, most observers can accept that the interaction they are witnessing is legitimate and true. As described above, this allows individual stakeholders to overcome their natural resistance to change. In much the same way, the team can collectively set aside its political infighting and unite behind the common goal of benefiting the customer. The shared experience of watching customers allows the team to form a consensus.

This is in fact what happened at the Gateway listening labs. Over two days of research, the attending executives progressed through a range of reactions: at first questioning the validity of the initial customers' feedback, then later—after seeing the pattern repeated for two days—accepting the feedback. Just as important was the stakeholders' consensus about changing the website. When we presented our recommendations for the redesign, the executives didn't have to be convinced but instead wanted to get started. Without the listening labs, it would have been nearly impossible for the team to form that consensus.

MOTIVATING THE TEAM TO ACT

The question remains how a consensus formed at listening labs can translate into tangible actions once the stakeholders are back at their desks. After all, a process that creates only intellectual agreement is unlikely to have much effect.

I've heard, for example, stories from companies that have hired "innovation firms" to conduct brainstorming sessions on behalf of the client. These tend to generate flashy PowerPoint decks that create momentary excitement that rapidly fades once the meeting is over. Without a more substantial basis for getting executive buy-in, deliverables like this—no matter how innovative—are unlikely to have much lasting effect.

Listening labs, by contrast, can spur stakeholders to take real action. The key is to get all the stakeholders into one room and physically show them the person they're supposed to be helping. I've found this human connection to be a uniquely powerful catalyst in motivating executives to enact change.

Listening labs consistently show that, contrary to the myth of the cold, profit-minded corporation, the business world has deep, untapped reserves of empathy. Most executives, regardless of their industry or role, have a strong desire to make a positive difference in customers' lives—yet the demands of schedule, office, and career conspire to prevent this from happening. Whether working within their silo, managing their team, or fighting political battles, most executives don't get much opportunity to be around customers. They need someone to invite them, and to urge them, to make the time to attend research.

Bring a group of busy executives to a day of listening labs and you're likely to see, by the end of the research, a very different side to those same people. I have often heard from clients that they feel a new connection to their customers because of the labs. One executive memorably told me, following his first time attending labs, that he could only compare the experience to "the moon shot." The labs had opened for him the vast possibility and potential in a customer-inclusive mindset.

There are, of course, other methods that can bring stakeholders together. Yet they typically don't have the kind of impact that we see at listening labs. For instance, many common research methods (as covered in Chapters 4 and 5) ask for opinions instead of behavior, use predefined tasks limiting the scope of the insights, or invent reactions from fictional characters. Decision makers are less likely to feel a connection to customers in those contexts.

Another increasingly popular way that some teams attempt to involve the organization is the brainstorming session, often billed as an innovation or "design thinking" workshop. I'll grant that stakeholders indeed are engaged in the process. Whether going to a whiteboard to sketch big thoughts, or bending pipe-cleaners to fashion a new gadget, people in these workshops are undoubtedly having more fun than they would at a listening lab, hearing customers bring up difficult truths. Treated purely as a team-building exercise these activities are harmless, but they're no substitute for good customer research revealing unmet needs. (Conducted after such research, however, brainstorming exercises can be invaluable in beginning the design process.)

The real value of listening labs—why they generate such good findings, enable consensus, and motivate action—is in their very design. Listening labs are about the *customer*, not the moderator or the method. Those aspects are present, of course, but labs are designed to put customers and their experience front and center, while the supporting items stay quietly in the background. This is why listening labs are so effective with warring political factions. The truth, whether it's good or bad news, is delivered by the one person all stakeholders can believe in: the customer.

I'll conclude with the caveat that listening labs are just the particular method we have found helpful at Creative Good. As shown in the next chapter, there are plenty of inspirational leaders who have succeeded by including the customer in other ways.

CHAPTER 9 SUMMARY

Encouraging an organization to include the customer is made difficult by stakeholders' natural resistance to change. This chapter shows how listening labs can overcome those obstacles.

KEY POINTS

- If you want a customer experience project to succeed, the single most important thing you can do is invite the decision makers to attend the research.
- The "Gunfire at Sea" case study explains why organizations avoid change, even when the change would greatly benefit the organization.
- Listening labs are designed to put customers and their experience front and center.
- The customer is the one person who can reliably cut through individual resistance and internal political conflict. Getting stakeholders to watch customers together can pave the way toward consensus.

10

THE ROLE OF LEADERS

"I want to hear it all."

D avid Neeleman is best known for founding JetBlue, the airline
that achieved early success with a customer-friendly approach.
Neeleman went on to start a Brazilian airline named Azul, whose
rapid growth prompted *Fortune* to call it "the next JetBlue." In a 2012
interview he spoke at length about his work. Of all his responsibilities
and tasks as CEO, Neeleman said, his favorite activity is "to get on
airplanes and talk to customers." He continued:

> Every flight I take, I go through the cabin [and] say, please
> give me your complaints, your compliments, I want to
> hear it all. I learn a lot of things from talking to customers.

> And I make every single vice president and director of our
> company do the exact same thing. When they're on a flight,
> they need to talk to customers. [If] you sit in your office
> all day you become stale, you don't really understand your
> business. Especially in Brazil, people don't like to give you
> bad news, they like to hide stuff a little bit. I want everyone
> to be open. I can't fix something if I don't know it's broken.

It's natural for executives to want to avoid bad news; it stems
from the resistance to change discussed in the previous chapter.
The most reliable source of negative feedback is usually customers

themselves. As David Neeleman demonstrates, the best leaders—
and by extension, the best companies—don't avoid hearing bad news
from customers. Instead, they not only listen to what customers have
to say, they actively seek it out. (Charlie Munger shares a standing rule
that he and Warren Buffett have at Berkshire Hathaway: "Always tell
us the bad news promptly. It is only the good news that can wait.")
Anyone with an interest in "hearing it all" or getting "the bad news
promptly" should spend time with customers.

Neeleman's remark reveals three signs of an organization that
successfully includes its customers. First, the CEO is prepared to act,
whether to "fix something" (as Neeleman put it) or otherwise make
some change that helps deliver a superior customer experience. As
I pointed out earlier, a customer-inclusive worldview can be judged
only by its tangible results. By spending time around customers,
Neeleman shows that he is not simply giving lip service to the idea of
including customers but is willing to take action.

Second, the CEO sets the expectation that senior executives will
get out from behind their desks and spend time with customers.
This delivers the message that the customer experience is everyone's
job, not just the CEO's, and thus helps foster a corporate culture that
values customer input.

Finally, *it's the CEO doing all of this.* Neeleman leads the way, setting
the example for the rest of his organization. This fits a distinct pattern
I've seen in the hundreds of consulting engagements that Creative
Good has run. The single most important predictor of success, for
any "customers included" initiative, is the participation of leadership.
Whether it's the product manager, chief marketing officer, or indeed
the CEO, any executive champion who leads the way in including
customers is setting the foundation for long-term success. The next
case study shows this kind of commitment.

DANNY MEYER AND HOSPITALITY

One of the most inspirational case studies of including the customer
comes from Danny Meyer, whom the *New York Times* called "the
greatest restaurateur Manhattan has ever seen." (Meyer has since

expanded well beyond Manhattan. His burger chain, Shake Shack, has locations across the U.S. and internationally, and went public in 2015.) Meyer's success stems from a customer-inclusive worldview that he explains in his outstanding book *Setting the Table*, which is essential reading for anyone interested in the customer experience.

In his book, Meyer describes a formative experience he had early in his career. While living in Rome, he observed that "the trattorias possessed a subtle quality that was every bit as important as the food: a genuinely welcoming spirit." This insight strongly influenced Meyer's concept for Union Square Cafe, his first restaurant, which combined skilled service and great cooking with "caring, gracious hospitality." During a time when fine dining in New York tended to be stuffy and traditional, Meyer's welcoming attitude propelled Union Square Cafe to almost immediate success.

Meyer goes on to explain both how to deliver a good experience to customers (whom he calls "guests") and how to motivate the organization to do so. The key, to use Meyer's language, is "hospitality," which he defines simply as "being on the guests' side." For example, the reservation desk shouldn't abruptly turn people away when the restaurant is fully booked, as many New York restaurants do. Instead, the reservationist should show that he or she is "rooting" for the customer and suggest an alternate time. Once guests are at the table, staff should avoid superficial or ostentatious displays of "service" and instead think about the experience from the guests' perspective. As Meyer puts it, "Anything that unnecessarily disrupts a guest's time with his or her companions or disrupts the enjoyment of the meal undermines hospitality."

At various points Meyer describes hospitality as an "athletic" pursuit which can come in two forms: "on offense" means finding "creative ways to enhance an already good experience," while "playing defense" means "overcoming mistakes or defusing situations guests [are] angry about." In all respects, hospitality is not a monologue but a "dialogue": "To be on a guest's side requires listening to that person with every sense, and following up with a thoughtful, gracious, appropriate response."

Meyer writes passionately about the importance of hiring, training, and managing the team that will be responsible for delivering the customer experience. The team is so important, Meyer writes, that in order for a culture of hospitality to thrive, customers must actually take *second* priority. Employees come first. Meyer says that "the guiding principal for practically every decision we make" is the careful prioritization of stakeholders: employees first, then customers (guests), followed by the community, suppliers, and investors. (Interestingly, David Neeleman reports learning the same lesson from another customer-inclusive leader, Herb Kelleher, the co-founder of Southwest Airlines: "Don't think about shareholders. Think about crew members. The crew will take care of the customers. The customers will take care of the shareholders.")

For Meyer, it all starts with assembling the right team. "The trick to delivering superior hospitality," Meyer writes, is "to hire genuine, happy, optimistic people." Those people have to be chosen carefully, because some things can't be taught:

> The overarching concern to do the right thing well [i.e., deliver hospitality] is something we can't train for. Either it's there or it isn't. So we need to train how to *hire* for it . . . It's not hard to teach anyone the proper way to set a beautiful table. What is impossible to teach is how to care deeply about setting the table beautifully.

While certainly not opposed to hiring happy, optimistic employees, most companies don't recruit with these exact criteria in mind—which raises an important question: Is it realistic to expect an organization to develop a customer-inclusive culture, if people aren't hired for "caring deeply" about the topic? My answer is yes. I've found that most people have a natural willingness and ability to care about customers but simply have never been asked to do so. More than one hard-nosed executive, after attending their first-ever day of listening labs, have reported that observing labs was the most transformative experience they had had in years. Whether in a structured context like listening labs, or more informally as Neeleman suggests, getting executives in front of customers can bring about an empathic impulse they never knew they had.

Meyer's focus on hospitality—both in his hiring, and toward his guests—offers a perfect case study of an organization exercising the "customers included" mindset over the long term. The results have been exceptional. Meyer was awarded the prestigious James Beard award in 2008 for Outstanding Restaurateur (although the more significant moment that night, he writes, was his son calling Shake Shack "the best restaurant in the world"). His restaurants have garnered top ratings from the *New York Times*, Zagat, Michelin, and other prominent reviewers; and except for one closure, every restaurant he has ever opened in over twenty-five years is still in business. Hospitality works.

CEOS AND THE LONG-TERM COMMITMENT

The organizations most likely to include customers are the ones with a CEO who is enthusiastic about doing so. The CEO sets the example and the expectation for other leaders in the organization to include the customer. Consider how the case studies of customer-inclusive organizations show active leadership from the chief executive:

- Steve Jobs brought Apple from the brink of bankruptcy to a pinnacle of success by explicitly focusing the company's overall strategy on the customer experience.
- Reed Hastings saved his company by focusing it on delivering the "fundamentals"—i.e., the basics that are most important in the Netflix customer experience.
- Tom Lee led the way in building a primary care network focused on fixing the systemic problems in the patient experience.
- David Neeleman set the example of caring about customers and seeking out the "bad news" that would help him improve the customer experience.
- Danny Meyer hired a team of "genuine, happy, optimistic" employees who could deliver hospitality to restaurant guests.
- Tupper Thomas made time to be around park visitors, find out what they wanted, and then fight for the changes that improved their experience.

In each case, the CEO (or its equivalent) accomplished all three steps in the "customers included" process: directly observing customers, discovering their unmet needs, and getting the entire organization behind the effort. The value of this approach is demonstrated by Apple, Netflix, One Medical, JetBlue, Danny Meyer's restaurants, and Prospect Park. It is no accident that these organizations have succeeded while other technology companies, health care organizations, airlines, and restaurants have struggled or failed. This is the benefit of the "customers included" worldview: *Given a competitive environment, in the long run, the best customer experience will eventually win.*

Unfortunately, many companies don't fit the mold described above. Some organizations are led by executives who are more interested in short-term gains than long-term investment. Others operate in a non-competitive environment and face little consequence for treating customers poorly. (It's no coincidence that of the ten worst-rated companies in a recent American Consumer Satisfaction Index, four are cable companies.) I can state a corollary to the principle above: *A poor customer experience indicates an organizational culture that is either short-term focused, non-competitive, or otherwise unaccustomed to including customers.* What's more, one can often judge an organization by the quality of the customer experience it creates. The next case study provides an example.

THE MICROSOFT STORY

Several years ago, one user got so fed up with his Windows PC that he wrote an angry email to the Windows team inside Microsoft. The user's name was Bill Gates.

"I am quite disappointed," wrote Gates in a 2003 email to several Microsoft employees, "at how Windows usability has been going backwards and the program management groups don't drive usability issues." Gates then described the reason for his email: he couldn't figure out how to download and install Microsoft's Moviemaker software on his Windows PC. Here are some highlights:

> The first 5 times I used the site it timed out while trying to bring up the download page. Then after an 8 second delay

I got it to come up. This site is so slow it is unusable . . . .

In fact it is more like a puzzle that you get to solve. It told me to go to Windows Update and do a bunch of incantations. This struck me as completely odd. Why should I have to go somewhere else and do a scan to download Moviemaker? . . .

So after more than an hour of craziness and making my programs list garbage and being scared and seeing that Microsoft.com is a terrible website I haven't run Moviemaker and I haven't got the plus package. The lack of attention to usability represented by these experiences blows my mind.

Gates was on fire; the user experience was awful. The real significance of the email, though, is in what happened next. One of the recipients of Gates' email, Will Poole, forwarded it to several other Microsoft employees, adding a brief introductory comment: "Guess we should start working on a list of things that need to be fixed." One of Poole's recipients, Amir Majidimehr, then added his own comment—"Can you guys coordinate?"—and forwarded it along to three more people. Gates' email was now three levels into the organization and no one had taken any responsibility for the problem, or for fixing it.

The email conversation reveals the challenges of business complexity described in the American Airlines case study. Gates had complained about several different applications, so it would have required the coordination of several internal teams to fully address his issues. Yet no one stepped up to lead the effort; if anything, the various stakeholders in the emails tried to pass to each other the ownership of the problem. While each stakeholder might have felt strongly about the usability of their one piece, there was a distinct lack of accountability on the team for the overall customer experience.

Thus, despite a strongly worded complaint from the boss, Microsoft couldn't muster the consensus, let alone the political will, to fix the glaring problems users faced. (In one email in the thread, one employee wrote that he wasn't sure how "to handle the complex mess of coordinating between product teams," the usability group, and the website team.) Whether it's a software user interface, the greeting at a restaurant, or the experience of practically any other product or service, how customers are treated is a direct reflection of the culture, and the inner workings, of the organization. Any organization that wants to include customers must have senior executives who will step up, take responsibility for the customer experience, and lead the rest of the team to do the same.

DILBERT ©2014 Scott Adams. Used by permission of UNIVERSAL UCLICK. All rights reserved.

HOW TO INCLUDE CUSTOMERS TOMORROW

Executives today have more distractions than ever, as the chaotic and quickly changing technology landscape has widespread effects on retail, finance, health care, media, entertainment, education, government, and every other sector and industry. The blistering speed of change tempts some executives to ignore customers in favor of a "shiny object," as Reed Hastings put it. Just keeping up with the trends is hard enough, whether it's the spread of mobile devices, the promise of big data, low-cost tech solutions lowering barriers to entry, shorter build cycles, or the current excitement for small, agile Internet startups.

But organizations are not well served by a strategy of chasing the latest buzzword or fad. In contrast, it's a customer-inclusive approach that enables long-term success. Looking at the world through this lens—taking the perspective of a customer—is an especially effective way of analyzing any new trend.

No matter what disruptions or buzzwords occur in tomorrow's environment, the "customers included" approach will take the same three steps:

1. *Observe customers directly.* Use a research method that reveals the full truth about the customer experience, rather than limiting yourself to tactical concerns or hypothetical findings. Observe what customers do, not merely what they say.

2. *Discover customers' unmet needs.* Find out what they need before you build something. Don't rely on the "spaghetti method" to happen upon the right idea by chance. And don't ask customers what they want. Go and find out.

3. *Get the organization involved.* Set the example for your team by spending time with customers. Run listening labs, if appropriate, and invite other stakeholders to attend. Be prepared to take action to create results.

This is not an academic exercise but real life, with real decisions, that affect real people. And it requires a long-term commitment. In a quickly changing environment, the primary challenge is to maintain an unwavering focus on serving customers. This is, after all, the job of the organization.

WHAT A COMPANY IS FOR

I'm making a bold claim. "Customers included" is not a one-off initiative for the team to try once in a while. Instead, I'm saying something bigger: including the customer is the ongoing responsibility of *any* company, *any* team, *any* organization. And like so many of the important concepts in this book, this is not a new idea. I'll return one last time to the great Peter Drucker, who explains not just why customers are important, but what a company actually *is*. In *The Practice of Management*, the classic 1954 book that practically invented the discipline of management, Drucker writes:

> There is only one valid definition of business purpose: to create a customer . . . What the customer thinks he is buying, what he considers "value," is decisive—it determines what a business is, what it produces, and

whether it will prosper. The customer is the foundation of a business and keeps it in existence.

Drucker expands the thought in his 1973 book, *Management*:

> With respect to the definition of business purpose and business mission, there is only one such focus, one starting point. It is the customer. The customer defines the business.

> A business is not defined by the company's name, statutes, or articles of incorporation. It is defined by the want the customer satisfies when he buys a product or service. To satisfy the customer is the mission and purpose of every business.

In other words, the very reason for the organization's existence is to create some benefit for that customer, to improve his or her life in some way. Including the customer is the basic essential ingredient in that process. Seen in this light, "customers included" is the very foundation on which any company or organization achieves lasting success. This goes for every company, non-profit organization, hospital, school, and government institution. And it goes for every type of customer: user, citizen, patient, student, and employee. *The ultimate goal of customer experience work is to improve people's lives.*

In the end, there is no one method for including customers. I've found listening labs to be effective in our client work, but other teams may find another method helpful. For example, Danny Meyer hires people for their hospitality instinct, while David Neeleman gets his executives to speak to passengers on airplanes. There are different paths to creating a good experience. What is common among all the approaches is that people on the team care enough about their customers to do the hard work of including them.

"Customers included" will become even more important in the coming years. The leaders of every industry, and every sector, will be those organizations, companies, and teams that practice this worldview. Keep an eye out for the health care company including patients, the government program including citizens, the non-profit including its beneficiaries, the company including its customers. These will be the organizations that will inevitably rise to the top, taking the lead, creating products and services that customers love, and producing significant and measurable impacts. This is work to be proud of, and I challenge you to try it. By including the customer, you might very well change the world.

ACKNOWLEDGMENTS

Since founding Creative Good in 1997, I've been fortunate to work with clients and colleagues who have taught me, and mentored me, as I developed the "customers included" approach. Many of those same people have helped directly on this book. I'm grateful for the support and encouragement of the entire Creative Good community: consulting clients, Gel attendees and speakers, newsletter readers, Good Todo users, and above all, the team.

I especially want to thank BJ Arnone, Andy Feldman, Cat Fitzgerald, Katie Pagenkopf, Elizabeth Peaslee, and Nicole Rubin for continuing to bring this vision to our clients. Thanks also to Phil Terry, who gave helpful feedback as I wrote the first edition of this book.

Several friends were helpful in guiding me throughout: Susan Danziger, Albert Wenger, Ken Trush, and David Bodanis. Thanks also to Terry Border for the cover image, and to Bill Keaggy and The Tremendousness Collective for the book design.

I'm grateful to the leaders, creators, and thinkers who teach us all how to include customers. I especially want to thank those featured in this book: Danny Meyer, Tom Lee, Alex Lee, Tupper Thomas, Reed Hastings, David Neeleman, Peter Morgan, and the late Steve Jobs, Elting Morison, and Peter Drucker.

Finally, a million thanks to my wife Ali, who put in countless hours editing this book (both editions!) and *Bit Literacy* before it. Ali, you and Max are still a joy every day.

Mark Hurst
Founder & CEO, Creative Good
mark@creativegood.com

New York City, March 2015

RECOMMENDED READING

H ere are a few standouts among the many books that inform the "customers included" perspective:

BUSINESS

Setting the Table, by Danny Meyer – as mentioned in Chapter 10, essential reading in which Meyer describes his customer-inclusive practice of "hospitality."

The Practice of Management, by Peter Drucker – the classic 1954 text on management, stating clearly for the first time "what a company is for." Drucker's 1973 book *Management: Tasks, Responsibilities, Practices* is a deep-dive into the topics covered in the earlier book, offering more detailed case studies (and more discussion of customers, especially in the first hundred pages).

Good Strategy, Bad Strategy, by Richard Rumelt – the single best book on strategy I'm aware of, describing a process that closely matches how Creative Good conducts strategy work.

Parkinson's Law, by C. Northcote Parkinson – an insightful and often hilarious look at how large organizations work.

Poor Charlie's Almanack, by Charlie Munger – a singularly important work covering a huge range of topics: behavioral science, ethics, investing, management, and more.

TECHNOLOGY

What Technology Wants, by Kevin Kelly – a sweeping account of technology and its effects throughout human history, and a helpful reminder that "technology" refers to a lot more than recent Internet trends.

Men, Machines, and Modern Times, by Elting Morison – the book that includes "Gunfire at Sea" (see Chapter 9) and much more, discussing how technology has changed, and been changed by, human society.

To Save Everything, Click Here, by Evgeny Morozov – an acerbic and provocative counterpoint to widespread hype about Internet technologies. While I don't agree with everything in the book, it's well worth reading to see a different perspective.

The Circle, by Dave Eggers – a dystopian novel about what happens to everyday people when digital technology becomes omnipresent.

Bit Literacy, by Mark Hurst – to be effective, executives today need to be able to manage their digital information. This book (my first) covers the basics of email, task management, and more.

NOTES

CHAPTER 1

9   **Los Angeles to Chicago is just over 2,000 miles:** Daniel Henniger, "America's Berlin Wall" (*Wall Street Journal*, June 20, 2013).

10   **major problems quickly became apparent:** Randolph C. Hite, "Testing and Problem Resolution Challenges Put Delivery of Technology Program at Risk" (U.S. Government Accountability Office, March 18, 2010). See also Richard M. Stana, "DHS Has Faced Challenges Deploying Technology and Fencing Along the Southwest Border" (U.S. Government Accountability Office, May 4, 2010).

10   **mistake windblown leaves, or even raindrops, for humans:** "Watching the Border: The Virtual Fence" (CBS News, January 2010): http://www.cbsnews.com/newswatching-the-border-the-virtual-fence/

11   **"an opportunity to provide feedback":** Richard M. Stana, "Observations on the Importance of Applying Lessons Learned to Future Projects" (U.S. Government Accountability Office, February 27, 2008).

11   **shut down SBInet in early 2011:** David Perera, "DHS cancels SBInet" (FierceGovernmentIT, January 14, 2011): http://www.fiercegovern-mentit.com/storydhs-cancels-sbinet/2011-01-14

11   **called the virtual fence "a complete failure":** Senate Hearing 111-1051, "Border Security: Moving Beyond the Virtual Fence" (U.S. Government Printing Office, April 20, 2010).Video: http://www.hsgac.senate.gov/hearings/border-security-moving-beyond-the-virtual-fence

11   **"It's a huge mistake":** "Watching the Border: The Virtual Fence" (CBS News, January 2010): http://www.cbsnews.com/news/watching-the-border-the-virtual-fence/

11   **"during its design and development":** Richard M. Stana, "Observations on the Importance of Applying Lessons Learned to Future Projects" (U.S. Government Accountability Office, February 27, 2008).

12   **"due to a compressed time frame":** Robert Pear, "Contractors Describe Limited Testing of Insurance Web Site" (*New York Times*, October 24, 2013).

12   **industry conference on border security:** "Raytheon Introduces Clear View™ Security Solutions at ASIS 2010" (Raytheon press release, October 11, 2010): http://raytheon.mediaroom.com/index. php?item=1664

12   **clearly aware of Boeing's troubles:** In addition to Raytheon, Boeing beat out Ericsson, Lockheed Martin, and Northrop Grumman to win the SBInet contract. See Alice Lipowicz, "Signed, sealed, delivered: Boeing gets SBI-Net" (*Washington Technology*, September 21, 2006): http://washingtontechnology.com/articles/2006/09/21/signed-sealed-delivered-boeing-gets-sbinet.aspx

12   **"thousands of pieces of ever-changing data":** Jacob Goodwin, "Raytheon's 'Clear View' system can keep a thousand eyes on the U.S. border" (*Government Security News*, October 17, 2010): http://www.gsnmagazine.com/node/21639?c=video_surveillance_cctv

12   **no mention of including the customer:** As of June 2013, SBInet was still being cited in national press as what not to do on the border. From Daniel Henninger, "America's Berlin Wall" (*Wall Street Journal*, June 20, 2013): "Anticipating that the immigration bill will provide several billion dollars of funding for a virtual border fence, defense contractors such as Northrop, General Atomics, General Dynamics and Lockheed Martin are hiring Beltway lobbyists to sell the government pilotless drones, advanced tracking technology, Apache helicopters and other post-Afghanistan inventory. This is a mistake." A year later, the government earmarked $145 million for another set of sensor towers, again in Arizona, this time built by a company called EFW. Raytheon filed a complaint when it wasn't awarded the job. See Aliya Sternstein, "Virtual Border Fence Project Halted After Raytheon Protest" (Nextgov.com, July 25, 2014): http://www.nextgov.com/defense/2014/07/Southwest-Virtual-Fence-Project-Halted-After-Raytheon-Protest/89705/

13   **the higher prices were described as a "terrific value":** Jessie Becker, "Netflix Introduces New Plans and Announces Price Changes" (Netflix blog, July 12, 2011): http://blog.netflix.com/2011/07/

netflix-introduces-new-plans-and.html . The price rose from $10 to $16 per month (this was for the standard DVD-and-streaming subscription).

13   **asking for donations to a "Netflix Relief Fund":** "Netflix Relief Fund with Jason Alexander" (Funny Or Die video, July 27, 2011): http://www.funnyordie.com/videos/15be7bfd8f/ netflix-relief-fund-with-jason-alexander

13   **a spinoff company named "Qwikster":** The email was also posted on the Netflix blog. Reed Hastings, "An explanation and some reflections" (Netflix blog, September 18, 2011): http://blog.netflix. com/2011/09/explanation-and-some-reflections.html

14   **several more new names for its service:** Kwickster, Qwickster, the_ REAL_netflix, Nutflix ("Do not go to Nutflicks, spelled this way. It's exactly what you think it is"), Qwakster, Nutqwakflikster, and Blockbus_ster. "Saturday Night Live," "Netflix Apology" (NBC, October 1, 2011): http://www.hulu.com/watch/284938 . See also The Oatmeal, a popular online comic by Matthew Inman, depicting Netflix as a misguided sandwich shop: http://theoatmeal.com/ comics/netflix

14   **"two websites would make things more difficult":** Reed Hastings, "DVDs will be staying at netflix.com" (Netflix blog, October 10, 2011): http://blog.netflix.com/2011/10/dvds-will-be-staying-at- netflixcom.html

14   **"depth of emotional attachment to Netflix":** Andrew Goldman, "Reed Hastings knows he messed up" (*New York Times Magazine*, October 20, 2011). See also William D. Cohan, "Seeing Red" (*Vanity Fair* website, February 22, 2012): http://www.vanityfair.com/ news/2012/02/netflix-201202

14   **canceled their accounts in a period of a few months:** Nick Wingfield and Brian Stelter, "How Netflix lost 800,000 members, and good will" (*New York Times*, October 24, 2011).

15   **a low of $54 about a year later:** Yahoo Finance shows a high of $298.73 on July 13, 2011 and a low of $53.80 on September 25, 2012: http://finance.yahoo.com/q?s=nflx

15   **saying his actions were "disruptive":** Farhad Manjoo, "Is Netflix as dumb as it seems?" (*Slate*, September 19, 2011): http://www.slate. com/articles/technology/technology/2011/09/is_netflix_as_dumb_ as_it_seems.html

16   **while ignoring the larger competitive landscape:** Clayton M. Christensen, *The Innovator's Dilemma: The Revolutionary Book That Will Change the Way You Do Business* (HarperBusiness, 1997), p. xviii.

16   **"it is right *not* to listen to customers":** Ibid., p. xv.

16   **easy interface that customers loved:** This is, in fact, what Netflix's strategy looks like in 2015.

16   **"arrogance based upon past success":** James B. Stewart, "Netflix Chief Looks Back on Its Near-Death Spiral" (*New York Times*, April 27, 2013).

17   **"embracing new technologies and adopting new business models":** A.W., "What disruptive innovation means" (*Economist* website, January 25, 2015): http://www.economist.com/blogs/economist-explains/2015/01/economist-explains-15

17   **the companies that were supposedly disrupted . . . are still active and profitable:** In a surprisingly defensive response, Christensen called Lepore's article a "criminal act of dishonesty." See Drake Bennett, "Clayton Christensen Responds to New Yorker Takedown of 'Disruptive Innovation'" (*Bloomberg Businessweek*, June 20, 2014): http://www.bloomberg.com/bw/articles/2014-06-20/clayton-christensen-responds-to-new-yorker-takedown-of-disruptive-innovation

17   **Christensen has repeatedly predicted that the iPhone would be disrupted:** Ben Thompson, "What Clayton Christensen Got Wrong" (Stratechery.com, September 22, 2013): http://stratechery.com/2013/clayton-christensen-got-wrong/ . On Christensen's contention that cheaper, "good enough" products will eventually disrupt more expensive alternatives, Thompson concludes: "The theory of low-end disruption is fundamentally flawed. . . It's time for the theory to change."

17   **attempts at disruption have a better chance of succeeding when they include the customer:** Christensen himself has written on this topic, encouraging companies to understand "the job customers want done." Carmen Nobel, "Clay Christensen's Milkshake Marketing" (*HBS Working Knowledge*, February 14, 2011): http://hbswk.hbs.edu/item/6496.html

18   **A "steady and disciplined" focus enabled Netflix to "execute on the fundamentals":** James B. Stewart, "Netflix Chief Looks Back on Its Near-Death Spiral" (*New York Times*, April 27, 2013).

CHAPTER 2

21 **as water gushed from a tap:** "South Africa: The Play Pump" (PBS website, October 24, 2005): http://www.pbs.org/frontlineworld/rough/2005/10/south_africa_th.html

22 *Time* **magazine column by former president Bill Clinton:** Bill Clinton, Laura Bush, and Jean Case, "How the New Philanthropy Works" (*Time* magazine, September 25, 2006).

22 **a video by** *National Geographic:* "National Geographic Feature on PlayPump Water Systems" (YouTube video, January 17, 2008): http://www.youtube.com/watch?v=uQu_Jppvzyk

22 **a concert in New York City:** "Timeline: The Playpump Trail / September to November 2006" (PBS website, undated): http://www.pbs.org/frontlineworld/stories/southernafrica904/timeline_tw.html

23 **to install for limited uses:** The Playpumps went to the non-profit Water For People. "Update on Playpumps technology," a post previously available on the Water For People website, suggested several improvements to the original Playpump model. For example, Playpumps should be "only installed in a school when provision [is] made for the community to have its own water point for general use."

23 **Owen Scott posted a five-minute video on YouTube:** "Playpump Vs. AfriDev" (YouTube video, April 8, 2010): http://www.youtube.com/watch?v=QRiNYmlAiIc

23 **"especially for the communities in need of water":** Karl Erpf and Ana Lucia Obiols, "Mission Report on the Evaluation of the PlayPumps installed in Mozambique" (Skat, April 29, 2008), p. 37. Available on the PBS website: http://www.pbs.org/frontlineworld/stories/southernafrica904/flash/pdf/mozambique_report.pdf . Skat's website: http://www.skat.ch/

24 **"leave the pump before getting dizzy":** Ibid., p. 24.

24 **"we want to try these here in Malawi":** Owen Scott, "The Playpump—A Review from Teachers" (Owen Scott's blog, August 18, 2010): http://barefooteconomics.ca/2010/08/18/the-playpump-a-review-from-teachers/

25 **"women are left spinning the wheel manually to draw water":** Owen Scott, "The Playpump IV—Playpump vs. AfriDev" (Owen Scott's blog, April 11, 2010): http://barefooteconomics.ca/2010/04/11/the-playpump-iv-playpump-vs-afridev/

25 **"and had never been repaired or replaced"**: "Troubled Water: Synopsis and Video" (PBS website, June 29, 2010): http://www. pbs.org/frontlineworld/stories/southernafrica904/video_index. html . The journalist, Amy Costello, was inspired by her experience reporting on the PlayPump to launch a podcast, Tiny Spark, on "investigating the business of doing good": http://www.tinyspark. org/blog/genesis/

26 **"implementation strategy lacks adequate community consultation"**: Clarissa Brocklehurst and Peter Harvey, "An Evaluation of the PlayPump® Water System as an Appropriate Technology for Water, Sanitation and Hygiene Programmes" (Unicef, October 2007). Available on the PBS website: http://www.pbs.org/frontlineworld/stories/southernafrica904/flash/pdf/unicef_pp_report.pdf . Strangely, the document is missing a page (p. 9) that includes part of a section on "Social Issues."

26 **"communicated through the press to first world audiences"**: Ralph Borland, "Radical Plumbers and Playpumps—Objects in Development" (Trinity College, Dublin, 2011): http://ralphborland. net/phd/index.html

27 **"the triumph of rich-country whimsy over poor-country relevance"**: Owen Scott, "The Playpump V—Response to Recent Publicity" (Owen Scott's blog, July 21, 2010): http://barefooteconomics. ca/2010/07/21/the-playpump-v-response-to-recent-publicity/

27 **a $99 soccer ball with an embedded chargeable battery**: Charles Kenny and Justin Sandefur, "Can Silicon Valley Save the World?" (*Foreign Policy*, July/August 2013).

27 **"innovation" has been so overused that it's not always clear what people mean**: The *Wall Street Journal* has noted that "most CEOs now spray the word 'innovation' as if it were an air freshener." For example, Kellogg CEO John Bryant announced as an "innovation" his company's new peanut butter flavored Pop-Tart. See Dennis K. Berman, "Is a Peanut Butter Pop-Tart an Innovation?" (*Wall Street Journal*, December 3, 2013).

27 **"most innovations are presumed to be self-evidently good"**: Evgeny Morozov, *To Save Everything, Click Here: The Folly of Technological Solutionism* (PublicAffairs, 2013), p. 167. Morozov also references the important work of Benoit Godin, some of whose research on the history of innovation is available here: http://www.csiic.ca/

28   **"sometimes they will work, other times they won't":** Jean Case, "The painful acknowledgement of coming up short" (Case Foundation blog, May 4, 2010): http://www.casefoundation.org/blog/painful-acknowledgement-coming-short

28   **measuring the results to find the best idea ("selection"):** This approach is nicely described in Tim Harford's book *Adapt: Why Success Always Starts with Failure* (Farrar, Straus and Giroux, 2011).

28   **the Silicon Valley adage to "fail early, fail often":** The mindset is illuminated in Nathaniel Rich, "Y Combinator, Silicon Valley's Start-Up Machine" (*New York Times Magazine*, May 2, 2013).

29   **"the consumer's or client's need for a significant change":** Peter F. Drucker, *Management: Tasks, Responsibilities, Practices* (HarperCollins, 1973), pp. 788 and 792.

29   **an existing pump in use since the 1930s:** The official name of Morgan's pump is the Zimbabwe bush pump 'B' type, as it was an improvement of the 'A' type designed by Tommy Murgatroyd in 1933. Peter Morgan, *Rural Water Supplies and Sanitation* (Ministry of Health, Zimbabwe, 1990), p. 153.

29   **construction could be improved (and made more cost-effective):** Morgan writes that the B type pump "retains the strength and durability of the old standard [A] model, but simplifies the pump head arrangement and reduces the capital and maintenance costs." Ibid., p. 160.

30   **"rather than introduce something foreign":** Ibid., p. 7.

30   **"as they do when they are involved":** Ibid., p. 106.

31   **"nothing without the community that it will serve":** Marianne de Laet and Annemarie Mol, "The Zimbabwe Bush Pump: Mechanics of a Fluid Technology" (*Social Studies of Science*, April 2000), p. 249.

31   **doesn't draw attention to itself:** A notable exception is that the bush pump was once featured on a Zimbabwe postage stamp. See Peter Morgan, "Manual: The Zimbabwe Bush Pump" (2009): http://www.clean-water-for-laymen.com/support-files/bushpumpmanual.pdf

32   **"waving his laptop in the air in excitement":** Michael Arrington, "What Just Happened? Thursday Was Supposed To Be Bing Day" (TechCrunch, May 28, 2009): http://techcrunch.com/2009/05/28/what-just-happened-thursday-was-supposed-to-be-bing-day/ . Video footage of the demo is shown in "Google Wave Developer Preview at Google I/O 2009" (YouTube video, May 28, 2009): http://www.youtube.com/watch?v=v_UyVmITiYQ

33   **"makes email look stale"**: MC Siegler, "Google Wave Drips With Ambition. A New Communication Platform For A New Web" (TechCrunch, May 28, 2009): http://techcrunch.com/2009/05/28/google-wave-drips-with-ambition-can-it-fulfill-googles-grand-web-vision/

33   **"more intuitive than email"**: Ben Parr, "Testing Google Wave: This Thing is Tidal" (Mashable, May 31, 2009): http://mashable.com/2009/05/31/google-wave-test/

33   **"redefine not only email, but the entire web"**: Ben Parr, "Google Wave is Coming: 100,000 Invites Go Out on September 30th" (Mashable, July 21, 2009): http://mashable.com/2009/07/21/google-wave-invites/

33   **"an extraordinary technical achievement"**: Ryan Paul, "Turning the tide: a hands-on look at Google's Wave" (Ars Technica, September 30, 2009): http://arstechnica.com/information-technology/2009/09/surfing-the-google-wave/

33   **"the worst of email and IM together: unproductivity"**: Robert Scoble, "Google Wave crashes on beach of overhype" (Scobleizer, October 1, 2009): http://scobleizer.com/?p=5929

34   **"like a Segway for email"**: Anil Dash (Twitter, October 2, 2009): https://twitter.com/anildash/status/4559430437 . Segways are, of course, those two-wheeled motorized scooters often used for sight-seeing tours. When the Segway was released, there were predictions that the device would revolutionize transportation and change the design of cities worldwide.

34   **"they'd have put in Jedi Knights and Klingons, too"**: Daniel Lyons, "Google Wave. Huh. What Is It Good For?" (*Newsweek*, October 15, 2009).

34   **"has not seen the user adoption we would have liked"**: Urs Hölzle, "Update on Google Wave" (Google Official Blog, August 4, 2010): http://googleblog.blogspot.com/2010/08/update-on-google-wave.html

34   **"the key experiential question of Google Glass isn't what it's like to wear them"**: Mark Hurst, "The Google Glass feature no one is talking about" (Creative Good blog, February 28, 2013): http://creativegood.com/blog/the-google-glass-feature-no-one-is-talking-about/

35   **the device was ridiculed on "Saturday Night Live"**: "Saturday Night Live," "Weekend Update: Randall Meeks Online" (NBC, May 4, 2013): http://www.hulu.com/watch/486603 . See also Greg Kumparak, "Saturday Night Live Takes On Google Glass"

(TechCrunch, May 5, 2013): http://techcrunch.com/2013/05/05/saturday-night-live-takes-on-google-glass/

35 **Google announced that it was halting sales of Google Glass altogether:** "We're graduating from Google[x] labs" (Google blog post, January 15, 2015): https://plus.google.com/+GoogleGlass/posts/9uiwXY42tvc?e=-RedirectToSandbox

35 **"This wasn't how the story was supposed to end":** Nick Bilton, "Why Google Glass Broke" (*New York Times*, February 4, 2015).

CHAPTER 3

37 **The customer is always right:** "How Stew Leonard's Customer Service Rock of Commitment Came to Be" (Stew Leonard's website, 2007 Press Releases).

38 **there's no evidence that Ford ever said that:** Patrick Vlaskovits, "Henry Ford, Innovation, and That 'Faster Horse' Quote" (HBR Blog Network, August 29, 2011): https://hbr.org/2011/08/henry-ford-never-said-the-fast

38 **"rarely wind up getting what they really want that way":** Bo Burlingham and George Gendron, "The Entrepreneur of the Decade" (*Inc. Magazine*, April 1, 1989).

38 **"People don't know what they want until you show it to them":** Andy Reinhardt, "Steve Jobs on Apple's Resurgence: 'Not a One-Man Show'" (*BusinessWeek*, May 12, 1998).

39 **"but to Mr. Jobs and a few members of his team":** Steve Lohr, "Can Apple Find More Hits Without Its Tastemaker?" (*New York Times*, January 18, 2011).

39 **"every button, every corner, every chime":** David Pogue, "Steve Jobs: Imitated, Never Duplicated" (*New York Times* website, October 6, 2011): http://pogue.blogs.nytimes.com/2011/10/06/steve-jobs-imitated-never-duplicated/

39 **"don't listen to your customers":** Leander Kahney, *Inside Steve's Brain* (Portfolio Hardcover, 2009), p. 65.

40 **"recorded by a third-grade teacher on Ambien":** David Pogue, "Take Back the Beep Campaign" (*New York Times* website, July 30, 2009): http://www.nytimes.com/2009/07/30/technology/personaltech/30pogue-email.html

40 **"It was just Byzantine":** Walter Isaacson, *Steve Jobs* (Simon & Schuster, 2011), p. 466.

41   **then creating a three-way conference call:** Footage of the demo is
      available in several YouTube videos (search for "iPhone 2007"). See
      also Peter Cohen, "Macworld Expo Keynote Live Update" (*Macworld*,
      January 9, 2007): http://www.macworld.com/article/1054764/live-
      update.html

41   **outselling the previous three months of *all* smartphones combined:**
      Michael Degusta, "Are Smart Phones Spreading Faster than Any
      Technology in Human History?" (*Technology Review*, May 9, 2012).

41   **"instead of one that the carriers approve of":** Fred Vogelstein, "The
      Untold Story: How the iPhone Blew Up the Wireless Industry"
      (*Wired*, February 2008).

42   **"we can leverage this experience people already have":** Walter
      Isaacson, *Steve Jobs* (Simon & Schuster, 2011), p. 127.

43   **"then how are we gonna market that":** Video footage of this
      moment is available in the YouTube video "Steve Jobs Insult
      Response" (uploaded on June 8, 2011): http://www.youtube.com/
      watch?v=FF-tKLISfPE

44   **"Steve didn't believe in that":** Leander Kahney, "John Sculley
      on Steve Jobs, The Full Interview Transcript" (Cult of Mac,
      October 14, 2010): http://www.cultofmac.com/63295/
      john-sculley-on-steve-jobs-the-full-interview-transcript/

44   **drop by the Apple Store in Palo Alto to peek in:** Steve Lohr, "Can
      Apple Find More Hits Without Its Tastemaker?" (*New York Times*,
      January 18, 2011).

44   **"peering inside to see what was going on":** Jeremy Britton, "Hiding
      in the Bushes with Steve Jobs" (ZURBlog, February 22, 2011): http://
      www.zurb.com/article/588/hiding-in-the-bushes-with-steve-jobs

44   **"We just can't ship junk":** "Steve Jobs: We don't ship junk" (YouTube
      video uploaded on April 29, 2008): http://www.youtube.com/
      watch?v=Yuoqeb_rJYU

45   **"the most profitable quarter of any company in history":** "iThrone"
      (*Economist*, January 31, 2015).

CHAPTER 4

52   **Malcolm Gladwell explained why:** Malcolm Gladwell, "The Ketchup
      Conundrum" (*New Yorker*, September 6, 2004).

53 **customers pronounced that its pizza tasted "like cardboard":**
Associated Press, "Domino's says new recipes, frank ad campaign
help double profit" (*USA Today*, March 2, 2010).

54 **"what you'd like to see online from a car company":** The events here
are depicted to the best of my memory, so these aren't exact quotes.

57 **"faster, friendlier and cleaner":** Teresa Lindeman, "Re-making
Wal-Mart" (*Pittsburgh Post-Gazette*, October 28, 2009). Throughout
the body text, for readability, I have standardized the spelling of the
company name to "Walmart," which is how the company spells
it today.

57 **called Project Impact:** Walmart 2010 Annual Report, p. 11:
http://stock.walmart.com/annual-reports

57 **That company was Target:** "John Fleming Named Wal-Mart's
Chief Marketing Officer" (Walmart, April 28, 2005):
http://news.walmart.com/news-archive/2005/04/28/
john-fleming-named-wal-marts-chief-marketing-officer

58 **"clear sight lines" throughout the store:** Jack Neff, "Walmart Makes Too
Much of an 'Impact', Beefs Up Assortment" (*Ad Age*, July 12, 2010).

58 **15% of the store inventory had vanished:** Pallavi Gogoi, "Walmart's
'Project Impact' Craters Sales, but the Retailer Persists" (DailyFinance,
March 31, 2010): http://www.dailyfinance.com/2010/03/31/
walmarts-project-impact-leaves-a-crater-in-sales-but-the-ret/

58 *positive* **growth in nearly every month during that time:** "State of US
Same-Store Sales—September 2010 and Quarterly Data Update and
Full-Year Outlook" (*Retailer Daily*, October 29, 2010).

59 **"And the customers love it":** "WMT—Wal-Mart Stores, Inc.
at Goldman Sachs Retailing Conference" (Thomson Reuters,
September 10, 2009).

59 **customers *say* they love the new stores:** Interestingly, Walmart executives continued to point to the survey data even as poor financial
results rolled in. In March 2010, Walmart COO Bill Simon said the
following at a Bank of America Merrill Lynch Consumer Conference:
"Fast, friendly, clean, is something that the store operations group
has spent a lot of time on and we're very happy that in the fourth
quarter we had the highest customer experience scores that we've
ever had . . . We survey customers. We get responses from about
500,000 customers a month . . . We track these every single month
and we've seen improvement every single month." Moments later,

Simon asserted that stores remodeled under Project Impact were seeing sales numbers of 125 to 150 basis points higher than non-remodeled stores, which seems at odds with Walmart's rollback of the strategy. See "WMT—Wal-Mart Stores, Inc. at Bank of America Merrill Lynch Consumer Conference" (Thomson Reuters, March 10, 2010): http://media.corporate-ir.net/media_files/irol/11/112761/Transcripts/Transcript20100310T1750.pdf

59 **"But they stopped shopping there":** Brian O'Keefe, "Meet the CEO of the biggest company on earth" (*Fortune*, September 9, 2010).

60 **left Walmart within a year:** Jack Neff, "Walmart Makes Too Much of an 'Impact', Beefs Up Assortment" (*Ad Age*, July 12, 2010).

60 **didn't get a single mention in the 2011 annual report:** Walmart's annual reports are available here: http://stock.walmart.com/annual-reports

60 **returning them to their original state:** Remodeling a single store cost millions of dollars. In the first year alone of Project Impact, Walmart planned to remodel over 500 of its several thousand stores. See Jack Neff, "Walmart's 'Project Impact' Redesign Takes Toll on Sales" (*Ad Age*, October 19, 2009).

60 **seven quarters in a row:** Stephanie Clifford, "U.S. Sales At Wal-Mart Show Decline" (*New York Times*, February 22, 2011). The earnings release is here: http://media.corporate-ir.net/media_files/irol/11/112761/quarterlyresults/4Q11_release.pdf . See also the transcript of the earnings announcement, in which CEO Mike Duke refers to "merchandise assortment and presentation issues": http://media.corporate-ir.net/media_files/irol/11/112761/Transcripts/4Q11_transcript.pdf

60 **There was no escaping the fact that Walmart had gotten hammered:** The business press did not let Walmart forget its mistake. When Mike Duke retired from Walmart in 2013, the *Wall Street Journal* ran a story summarizing his tenure as CEO, noting the "disastrous results" generated by Project Impact: see Shelly Banjo, "Wal-Mart Taps Veteran as New CEO" (*Wall Street Journal*, November 25, 2013).

61 **"features that are easy to verbalize may not be that important":** Barry Schwartz and Kenneth Sharpe, *Practical Wisdom: The Right Way to Do the Right Thing* (Riverhead, 2010), p. 86.

61 **many people immediately think of focus groups or surveys:** Recall the articles, written around the time of Steve Jobs' death, conflating market research with focus groups.

62　　**the embodiment of a team's own internal assumptions and beliefs:** See Nick De Voil, "Personas Considered Harmful" (De Voil Consulting, 2010): http://www.devoil.com/papers/PersonasConsideredHarmful. pdf

63　　**data sources to guide persona creation:** Tamara Adlin and John Pruitt, *The Essential Persona Lifecycle: Your Guide to Building and Using Personas* (Morgan Kaufmann, 2010), Kindle location 413.

63　　**"embedded knowledge" about customers:** Ibid., Kindle location 1055.

63　　**"Most businesses are not rocket science":** Ibid., Kindle location 1055.

63　　**a shock to executives who are accustomed to paying attention only to their personas:** See Steve Portigal, "Persona Non Grata" (*interactions*, January/February 2008) in which Portigal describes his encounter with a "persona doll," a little cardboard cutout representing a persona. Presumably this tangible artifact makes it easier for a team to project thoughts and assumptions onto an external personality. Portigal wonders why any company would want to personify its customers "as mere dolls, as dehumanized, lifeless, plastic lumps that are without will, motion, action, or emotion . . . there is powerful subtext here."

64　　**"evidence that should be critical to our judgment is missing":** Daniel Kahneman, *Thinking, Fast and Slow* (Farrar, Straus and Giroux, 2011), pp. 86 and 87.

CHAPTER 5

68　　**"We repeatedly had to pull over," they wrote of the incident:** Ben Stewart, "2013 Ford Fusion Test Drive" (*Popular Mechanics*, September 24, 2012).

68　　**"help consumers fall in love with their vehicles again":** "MyFord™ Defines a New Driver Experience" (Ford website, January 7, 2010): https://social.ford.com/content/fordsocial/en/articles/in-the-news/ ford-cars/my/3982-myforde284a2-defines-a-new-driver- experience.html

68　　**deemed it "intuitive and easy to use":** Tim Stevens, "MyFord dash and Sync App Ecosystem hands-on" (Engadget, January 7, 2010): http://www.engadget.com/2010/01/07/ myford-dash-and-sync-app-ecosystem-make-us-want-a-blue-oval/

68　　**"an unfortunate mess," citing the difficulty of using the maps feature:** Colum Wood, "2013 Ford Fusion Review" (AutoGuide.com, September 24, 2012): http://www.autoguide.com/manufacturer/

ford/2013-ford-fusion-review-video-2224.html . Note that this review, and the one in *Popular Mechanics*, were published after Ford's update to the touchscreen earlier in 2012. The original version of MyFord Touch was even more problematic.

68 **"All-in-all, it's an aggravating design":** Mike Quincy, "Test complete: 2011 Ford Edge" (*Consumer Reports*, January 14, 2011): http://www. consumerreports.org/cro/news/2011/01/test-complete-2011-ford-edge/index.htm

68 **"the frustrations of MyFord Touch even to an adversary":** "Why the MyFord Touch control system stinks" (*Consumer Reports*, August 22, 2012): http://www.consumerreports.org/cro/news/2012/08/why-the-myford-touch-control-system-stinks/index.htm

69 **"preset button without looking are gone,"** *Consumer Reports* **lamented:** Tom Mutchler, "MyFord/MyLincoln Touch: A touch of intuition, or insanity?" (*Consumer Reports*, December 8, 2010): http://news. consumerreports.org/cars/2010/12/myford-ford-edge-mylincoln-touch-lincoln-mkx-sync-a-touch-of-intuition-or-insanity.html

69 **News broke in early 2014 that Ford was abandoning the voice-recognition system:** Nick Wingfield and Jaclyn Trop, "Ford to Drop Microsoft From Car Systems" (*New York Times* website, February 24, 2014): http://bits.blogs.nytimes.com/2014/02/24/ford-to-drop-microsoft-from-car-systems/ . See also Chris Woodyard, "Ford dumping Microsoft to sync with BlackBerry" (*USA Today*, February 25, 2014).

69 **"a wreck," "a disaster," as well as some unprintable names:** When *Consumer Reports* posted a video about MyFord Touch to YouTube, Ford owners posted their reactions in the comments section. See "Frustrating MyFord Touch" (YouTube video, December 6, 2010): https://www.youtube.com/watch?v=H64QTs8qDfI

70 **might be "just too complicated":** Alisa Priddle, "MyFord Touch: Cutting edge, or just too complicated?" (*Detroit Free Press*, June 23, 2013). The results were better a year later, as Ford moved up to 16th place. "The reason it fell—issues with the MyFord Touch infotainment system—is the same reason it improved," reported the *Times*, noting that Ford had released a number of improvements. See Cheryl Jensen, "Porsche Tops J.D. Power Initial Quality Study for Second Consecutive Year" (*New York Times*, June 18, 2014).

70 **two members of the MyFord Touch design team shortly after the system launched:** Iain Roberts and Tasos Karahalios, "IDEO Case

Study: MyFord Touch" (Vimeo video uploaded September 26, 2010):
http://vimeo.com/15288071

71   **the cause remained a mystery:** Technically it was the copilot who
      managed the landing gear in the B-17. Here I use "pilot" to stand for
      pilot or copilot.

72   **the runway crashes stopped almost immediately:** Unfortunately,
      some planes didn't get the handles installed in time to prevent a
      crash. Here's a first-hand account of an incident that occurred two
      years after Chapanis's project: "In 1945, on Peleliu Island in the
      Western Pacific, I happened to be watching as a C-46 came in for
      a smooth landing on a coral runway, then appeared to settle under
      the surface like a submarine starting to submerge. There were
      sparks and an explosion . . . " Stanley N. Roscoe, "From the Roots
      to the Branches of Cockpit Design: Problems, Principles, Products"
      (*Human Factors Society Bulletin*, Vol. 35, No. 12, 1992).

73   **hundreds of wartime mishaps that were designated "pilot errors":** To
      clarify the service names: the U.S. Air Force was formed by an act of
      Congress in 1947, essentially replacing what had been the U.S. Army
      Air Forces. So while the bombers in question had flown World War
      II missions under AAF command, the Fitts and Jones reports were
      published by the Air Force.

74   **two reports on the topic . . . "designing equipment in accordance
      with human requirements":** Paul M. Fitts and R. E. Jones, "Analysis
      of Factors Contributing to 460 'Pilot-Error' Experiences in Operating
      Aircraft Controls" (U.S. Air Force, Aero Medical Laboratory, July 1,
      1947), and Paul M. Fitts and R. E. Jones, "Psychological Aspects of
      Instrument Display. I: Analysis of 270 'Pilot-Error' Experiences in
      Reading and Interpreting Aircraft Instruments" (U.S. Air Force, Aero
      Medical Laboratory, October 1, 1947). Both are reprinted in Wallace
      Sinaiko (ed.), *Selected Papers on Human Factors in the Design and Use
      of Control Systems* (Dover Publications, 1961).

74   **getting the pilots' stories, without judgement or leading questions:**
      I'm simplifying a little for brevity's sake. Some pilots were interviewed
      one-on-one, some were interviewed in a group, and hundreds more
      were invited to complete a written form containing the questions. All
      forms were submitted anonymously, so that pilots were able to relate
      their experiences more freely. Fitts and Jones describe the research
      method in their July 1947 report (see previous note), pp. 6-7.

75   **the cockpit design problems might never have surfaced:**
      Unfortunately, when a system fails due to bad interface design, it's

not uncommon for the human operator to be scapegoated. Sidney Dekker, who has written widely on the topic, calls this "the old view of human error"—blaming the human without taking into account the rest of the system. He argues that the 1947 research by Fitts and Jones "laid . . . the groundwork for the new view to human error," which takes into account the design of the system used by the operator. Sidney Dekker, "The re-invention of human error" (Lund University School of Aviation, Technical Report 2002-01).

75   **"were very experienced aviators":** L. F. E. Coombs, *Control in the Sky: The Evolution & History of the Aircraft Cockpit* (Pen and Sword Aviation, 2005), pp. 148-149.

75   **design decisions to be made "almost by default":** Stanley N. Roscoe, "From the Roots to the Branches of Cockpit Design: Problems, Principles, Products" (*Human Factors Society Bulletin*, Vol. 35, No. 12, 1992). The "default" was, in large part, to design the cockpit for the benefit of the construction process: the position of switches, dials, and other elements would be heavily influenced by the structure of the underlying wiring, hydraulics, and physical supports. The reason why different bombers had landing-gear switches in different places may very well have been because they had different wiring configurations.

76   **and strafed the school:** The trigger has two "detents," or positions, to activate its two functions. This is similar to the button on some digital cameras, which can be pushed halfway down to focus, or fully down to snap the photo. On the joystick trigger, the halfway-down position activates the jet's laser-driven targeting pod, which helps locate the target. To actually fire a weapon requires squeezing the trigger a bit harder. Assuming the right combat mode is activated, doing so activates the F-16's six-barreled, air-cooled General Electric M61 Vulcan machine gun. Be careful with that trigger: the gun fires a hundred rounds per second.

76   **The first item is "pilot error":** "Executive Summary: Aircraft Accident Investigation, F-16C, S/N 85-1474 Mishap" (Accident Investigation Board, U.S. Air Force, November 3, 2004): http://usaf.aib.law.af.mil/ ExecSum2005/F-16C_LittleEggHarbor_3Nov04.pdf . Available via "U.S. Air Force, Class A Aerospace Mishaps, Fiscal Year 2005": http://usaf.aib.law.af.mil/indexFY05.html . For a civilian incident report, see D'Vera Cohn and Allan Lengel, "D.C. Guard Jet Fires, Hitting N.J. School" (*Washington Post*, November 5, 2004). Two years later the Air Force reached a settlement to pay the school over half a million dollars. "N.J. school strafed by F-16 to get $519,070"

(Associated Press, November 1, 2006): http://www.msnbc.msn.com/id/15519398/ns/us_news-military/t/nj-school-strafed-f--get/

76 **Fitts and Jones' research methods weren't more fully adopted:** Still, Fitts went on to have a long career in the usability field. Any human-factors grad student can tell you about the law named after him. As Wikipedia puts it, Fitts' Law "predicts that the time required to rapidly move to a target area is a function of the ratio between the distance to the target and the width of the target." From "Fitts' law" (Wikipedia, retrieved February 23, 2015): http://en.wikipedia.org/wiki/Fitts_law

77 **"capability for data processing," and others:** H. Wallace Sinaiko and E. P. Buckley, "Human Factors in the Design of Systems" (NRL Report 4996, Naval Research Laboratory, August 29, 1957). Reprinted in Wallace Sinaiko (ed.), *Selected Papers on Human Factors in the Design and Use of Control Systems* (Dover Publications, 1961).

77 **"personnel subsystems" . . . commonly used research methods:** J. Keenan, T. Parker, and H. Lenzycki, "Concepts and Practices in the Assessment of Human Performance in Air Force Systems" (Aerospace Medical Research Laboratories, September 1965): http://www.dtic.mil/dtic/tr/fulltext/u2/625041.pdf . The report isn't only about task analysis, as it also includes mentions of checklists, surveys, questionnaires, and other familiar methods. Even inter-views—both "structured and unstructured"—get a mention, though the authors note that "the validity of the interview as a systematic means of collecting data has been questioned." Task-based research is clearly the preferred method.

77 **"He's a nonlinear machine":** Ibid., although that source was itself quoting Alphonse Chapanis, "The Design and Conduct of Human Engineering Studies" (San Diego State College Foundation, 1956).

77 **now the *tasks* were the focal point of user research:** An exception from that period is the Critical Incident Technique, which resembled a more structured version of Fitts and Jones' interviews. Developed by John Flanagan while he worked in the Army Air Force's Aviation Psychology Program, the method had users document notable incidents, good or bad, after they occurred. This was not concerned with measuring the success of a task so much as understanding the circumstances under which it had succeeded or failed. See John C. Flanagan, "The Critical Incident Technique" (Psychological Bulletin, Vol. 51, No. 4, July 1954): http://www.apa.org/pubs/databases/psycinfo/cit-article.pdf . Wikipedia also has a summary.

77   **Task-based usability had arrived:** One could trace the roots of this thinking even further back. The industrial-era motion studies of Frank and Lillian Gilbreth (who inspired *Cheaper by the Dozen*) observed factory workers and recommended improvements to their efficiency. The Gilbreths, in turn, were influenced by Frederick Winslow Taylor's work. For that matter, one could go all the way back to ancient Greece, where Hippocrates (460-370 BC) was already writing about ergonomics (see "Kat' Ihtreion," or "About the hospital").

78   **now billions—of people have interacted with user interfaces:** While task-based methods were certainly dominant in the early software era, a more in-depth history would reveal a kaleidoscope of perspectives among researchers at that time. A helpful source along these lines is John M. Carroll, "Human-Computer Interaction: Psychology as a Science of Design" (Virginia Tech, 1997). The paper describes a wide variety of research on software user interfaces occurring as early as the 1970s, including qualitative studies that resemble the more open-ended research that Creative Good runs. An even earlier work describing similar methods is the classic 1955 book *Designing for People* by industrial designer Henry Dreyfuss.

CHAPTER 6

82   **an annual fee of a couple hundred dollars:** Full disclosure: my family includes patients of One Medical. I was also quoted in this *New York Times* article about One Medical: Katie Hafner, "Concierge Medical Care With a Smaller Price Tag" (*New York Times*, January 31, 2011).

82   **well positioned to change how primary care is delivered:** Lee is an entrepreneur and physician who achieved success early in his career with a software product called Epocrates.

82   **"I still don't know the results":** "Tom Lee (founder, One Medical) at Gel 2011" (Vimeo video by the Gel conference, uploaded July 14, 2011): http://vimeo.com/26421646 . Transcript edited slightly for clarity.

83   **"big gap between concept and reality in customer experience":** Conversation with Tom Lee, July 22, 2013.

84   **"the leader and the pacesetter":** Peter F. Drucker, *Management: Tasks, Responsibilities, Practices* (HarperCollins, 1973), pp. 91-92.

85   **a surprising range of landscapes and vistas:** Vaux and Olmsted designed Prospect Park shortly after they designed Central Park.

85 **"controlling circumstances of the street of the town":** Witold Rybczynski, *A Clearing In The Distance: Frederick Law Olmsted and America in the 19th Century* (Scribner, 2000), p. 271, quoting Vaux and Olmsted's "Preliminary Report to the Commissioners for Laying Out a Park in Brooklyn."

86 **barracks and anti-aircraft batteries on park land:** Elliot Willensky, *When Brooklyn Was The World 1920-1957* (Harmony Books, 1986), p. 210.

86 **bringing Prospect Park back to life:** Kareem Fahim, "Returning Prospect Park to the People" (*New York Times*, April 5, 2010).

88 **when Thomas had arrived thirty years before:** Kareem Fahim, "Returning Prospect Park to the People" (*New York Times*, April 5, 2010).

88 **boutiques that accompany gentrification:** Park Slope, the neighborhood running along the west side of the park, became particularly well-known for a different kind of recent arrival: babies. On a typical summer afternoon in 2010, the park's Grand Army Plaza entrance was flooded with dozens of strollers weaving through the crowd. In a strange irony, Prospect Park's social scene had at last fully returned—with the attention focused, once again, on the people in the carriages.

92 **"Discover the Prospect Park you don't know":** Andy Geller, "B'klyn Park is Full of Prospects" (*New York Post*, March 26, 2008).

93 **"innovation, credit, advertising, or salesmanship" created it:** Peter F. Drucker, *Management: Tasks, Responsibilities, Practices* (HarperCollins, 1973), p. 61. Drucker's exact words, after listing the various types of unmet needs, are: "In every case, it is business action that creates the customer." Here Drucker uses "business" to stand for any company, organization, or institution. Similarly, Drucker uses "customer"—as I do throughout this book—to refer to any kind of end user of a product or service: consumer, citizen, patient, student, etc.

94 **as OXO and Smart Design discovered during research:** As Alex Lee pointed out during his Gel presentation, this was not a typical OXO project, as the company usually sources its product ideas internally. Still, I find the research findings instructive: users who clearly demonstrated their unmet need were unable to articulate it.

96 **method that closely resembles Lean:** Agile, Scrum, and Extreme Programming are three methods, typically associated with software development, that share some of Lean's characteristics. (Wikipedia has the details.)

97   **"iterating with customers as rapidly as possible":** Eric Ries, *The Lean Startup: How Today's Entrepreneurs Use Continuous Innovation to Create Radically Successful Businesses* (Crown Business, 2011), p. 250.

97   **"core advantage" of Lean teams:** Ibid., p. 252.

97   **describes this exact situation:** Jeff Gothelf with Josh Seiden, *Lean UX: Applying Lean Principles to Improve User Experience* (O'Reilly Media, 2013), pp. 102-105.

99   **the Sienna case study:** Eric Ries, *The Lean Startup: How Today's Entrepreneurs Use Continuous Innovation to Create Radically Successful Businesses* (Crown Business, 2011), pp. 86-88.

CHAPTER 7

103   **an unusual experience he had one day at lunch:** Nick Bilton, "Why Facebook Works for All, Twitter for Some" (*New York Times* website, September 27, 2011): http://bits.blogs.nytimes.com/2011/09/27/why-facebook-works-for-all-twitter-for-some/

CHAPTER 8

119   **"permanently destroying the brand and image" of the airline:** Dustin Curtis, "Dear American Airlines" (dustincurtis.com, posted May 18, 2009, no longer available online).

120   **the very first homepage of Expedia:** I partnered with Robert Seidman to create and publish the report. It's still online: http://www.goodexperience.com/reports/isoe/

122   **"a lot of tentacles that reach into a lot of interests":** Dustin Curtis, "Dear Dustin Curtis" (dustincurtis.com, posted May 31, 2009, no longer available online). The email from Mr. X was shown with a date of May 18, 2009, the day of Curtis's original post.

122   **management identified the employee and promptly fired him:** Tom Chivers, "American Airlines worker fired for replying to web user complaint" (*The Telegraph*, November 9, 2009): http://www.telegraph.co.uk/travel/travelnews/6531610/American-Airlines-workerfired-for-replying-to-web-user-complaint.html

123   **clueless leadership at American Airlines:** Dustin Curtis, "The Incompetence of American Airlines & the Fate of Mr X" (dustin-curtis.com, posted November 4, 2009, no longer available

online). Over three years later Curtis was still steamed, posting on Twitter that "American Airlines is by far the worst airline in the world" (Twitter, December 27, 2012): https://twitter.com/dcurtis/status/284186858181779457

125 **"those with the most power affecting the final choices":** Jeffrey Pfeffer, *Power: Why Some People Have It and Others Don't* (HarperBusiness, 2010), p. 224.

125 **how to "network with the right people":** Ibid., pp. 86 and 116.

126 **"thought her efforts were doomed":** Ibid., pp. 164 and 166.

126 **"particularly those she saw thwarting her efforts":** Ibid., pp. 172 and 166.

CHAPTER 9

129 **his classic essay "Gunfire at Sea":** Elting E. Morison, *Men, Machines, and Modern Times* (MIT Press, 1966), pp. 17-44.

132 **"half-eaten-away by cockroaches":** Ibid., p. 29.

132 **"blunter minds and less resilient imaginations":** Ibid., p. 35.

133 **changing their . . . "physical accommodations, conventions, and rituals":** Ibid., p. 36.

133 **the "normal human instinct to protect oneself":** Ibid., p. 36.

137 **"his own values, his own wants, his own reality":** Peter F. Drucker, *Management: Tasks, Responsibilities, Practices* (HarperCollins, 1973), p. 80.

137 **a typical day includes eight to ten one-on-one sessions:** This is just for facility-based listening labs. Field research, of course, can't fit that many sessions into one day. Visiting users' homes, offices, or meeting them for research in public adds travel time, not to mention the challenges of scheduling at multiple venues. Field research thus usually stretches across multiple days for a single customer segment.

138 **"irritations that tend to divide a top-management group":** Peter F. Drucker, *Management: Tasks, Responsibilities, Practices* (HarperCollins, 1973), p. 79.

138 **a 2004 paper about the "failure of deliberation":** Cass R. Sunstein, "Group Judgments: Deliberation, Statistical Means, and Information Markets" (University of Chicago Law School, August/October 2004): http://www.law.uchicago.edu/files/files/219-crs-groups-new.pdf

139 **"dissenting opinions to percolate up through the agency's hierarchy":** Columbia Accident Investigation Board, "NASA—Report of Columbia Accident Investigation Board, Volume I" (NASA, 2003), p. 183: http://www.nasa.gov/columbia/home/CAIB_Vol1.html

139 **"with the predeliberation tendencies of their members":** Cass R. Sunstein, "Group Judgments: Deliberation, Statistical Means, and Information Markets" (University of Chicago Law School, August/ October 2004): http://www.law.uchicago.edu/files/files/219-crs-groups-new.pdf

CHAPTER 10

145 **prompted *Fortune* to call it "the next JetBlue":** Patricia Sellers, "Azul: The next JetBlue" (*Fortune*, July 13, 2010): http://money.cnn.com/2010/07/13/news/companies/azul_neeleman_jetblue.fortune/index.htm

145 **"I can't fix something if I don't know it's broken":** "Kathleen Taylor and David Neeleman - Ideas Exchange - BBC" (YouTube video posted by the BBC on October 8, 2012): http://www.youtube.com/watch?v=tslllgLGNKs . Neeleman's quote starts around 11:40.

146 **"It is only the good news that can wait":** Charles T. Munger, *Poor Charlie's Almanack: The Wit and Wisdom of Charles T. Munger*, 2nd ed. (Donning, 2005), p. 452.

146 **"the greatest restaurateur Manhattan has ever seen":** *New York Times Magazine*, August 7, 2011, table of contents.

147 **"a genuinely welcoming spirit":** Danny Meyer, *Setting the Table: The Transforming Power of Hospitality in Business* (HarperCollins, 2006), p. 25.

147 **"caring, gracious hospitality":** Ibid., p. 61.

147 **"being on the guests' side":** Ibid., p. 11.

147 **"rooting" for the customer and suggest an alternate time:** Ibid., p. 57 and pp. 245-246.

147 **"disrupts the enjoyment of the meal undermines hospitality":** Ibid., p. 65.

147 **"defusing situations guests [are] angry about":** Ibid., p. 57. I've shortened the quote slightly for clarity.

148 **"The customers will take care of the shareholders":** Patricia Sellers, "Azul: The next JetBlue" (*Fortune*, July 13, 2010): http://money.cnn.

com/2010/07/13/news/companies/azul_neeleman_jetblue.fortune/
index.htm

148 **"to hire genuine, happy, optimistic people":** Danny Meyer,
Setting the Table: The Transforming Power of Hospitality in Business
(HarperCollins, 2006), p. 66.

148 **"how to care deeply about setting the table beautifully":** Ibid., pp. 142
and 144.

149 **calling Shake Shack "the best restaurant in the world":** Ibid., p. 315.

149 **in over twenty-five years is still in business:** For completeness
I should also note one sale: Meyer sold his high-end restaurant
Eleven Madison Park in 2011. See Glenn Collins, "Meyer Intends
to Sell Eleven Madison Park to Its Chef and Manager" (*New York
Times* website, October 4, 2011): http://dinersjournal.blogs.nytimes.
com/2011/10/04/meyer-intends-to-sell-eleven-madison-park-to-its-
chef-and-manager/ . As of this writing (March 2015), Eleven Madison
Park is still very much in business.

150 **four are cable companies:** Max Nisen, "The 15 Worst Companies For
Customer Service" (*Business Insider*, January 8, 2013): http://www.
businessinsider.com/15-worst-companies-for-customer-service-2013-1

150 **The user's name was Bill Gates:** Todd Bishop, "Full text: An epic Bill
Gates e-mail rant" (*Seattle Post-Intelligencer*, June 24, 2008).

151 **The real significance of the email, though, is in what happened next:**
As of March 2015, the PDF of the entire email thread is on the *Seattle
Post-Intelligencer* website: http://blog.seattlepi.com/microsoft/files/
library/2003Jangatesmoviemaker.pdf

154 **"the foundation of a business and keeps it in existence":** Peter F.
Drucker, *The Practice of Management* (HarperCollins, 1954), p. 37.

154 **"To satisfy the customer is the mission and purpose of every business":** Peter F. Drucker, *Management: Tasks, Responsibilities, Practices*
(HarperCollins, 1973), p. 79.

INDEX